PASTA
GRANNIES

COMFORT COOKING

Hardie Grant
BOOKS

VICKY
BENNISON

Welcome to the second volume of recipes and stories from Pasta Grannies! Back in 2015, when the YouTube channel first got going, my aim was to collect all the handmade pasta shapes to be found in Italy. That still is an objective, but the project has evolved. Six years later, people tune in for the Pasta, but stay for the Grannies. I didn't plan it this way, but the channel offers a double dose of comfort thanks to the cooking (of course) but, more importantly, the women we film. I know, because folks write and tell me. From the overwhelmed intensive care doctor who wants to be reminded that hard times will eventually pass, to the grandmother who makes the Friday video an event to be watched with her grandchildren, the Pasta Grannies' cheerfulness and resilience is a source of joy, solace and inspiration.

However, they are not cute. Here are ladies who remember a time before antibiotics became widely available, lived through the Second World War, had to grow or forage for food before it could be eaten, were manual labourers from an early age – all while cooking for their family. And they are still smiling. They know good food, cooked from scratch, nourishes not only the body but also our emotions – and creates connection whatever the weather or the times we live in.

Making pasta, through the decades and at the moment of creation, is meditative to do and soothing to watch. It is the antithesis of fast food and instant microwave fixes; it makes one slow down and focus on something we can create. And it reminds you of your own grandparents while creating your own traditions.

This book is a response to that affection. I've selected those recipes and episodes which are most popular with the two million of you who follow Pasta Grannies, the ones that you all find inviting and take most comfort from. This means you will find more than pasta dishes in this book. There are several *pasta al forno* – baked pasta – recipes, for example, because everyone loves a lasagna and its relatives; Maria and her pork and sage lasagna has been the top-viewed video for several years. Pasta means dough in Italian, and there's a chapter devoted to rustic pizza and crunchy pies. Rice recipes pop up all over Italy; who could say no to a creamy risotto or a large arancino, an oozy in the middle, deep-fried rice ball? And, of course, there are *dolci*, (desserts), such as the classic tiramisù with its origins in grannies treating their grandkids with a little whipped sugar and egg; and the lesser known – but decidedly moreish – buttery, fried apricot gnocchi. There is something for everyone: *Buon appetito!*

HOW TO MAKE PASTA BY HAND

The internet is full of rules about pasta-making and all the things that people get wrong; take no notice of these posts and articles, they are just creating barriers to enjoyment. Our *nonne* have been making pasta since they were children, so don't worry, it's not complicated. And sure, the first occasion you make pasta it might come out a little thick, or the pasta sheet might tear; but there is always next time, and it will still taste great even if you haven't managed to roll out a perfect circle of dough.

There are several pasta shapes you can make where the only tools you need are your hands – see gnocchi lunghi on page 52, for one example. For others, a few simple tools are required. These are some of the questions I'm most often asked about pasta-making kit:

WHY SHOULD I USE A WOODEN ROLLING PIN TO ROLL OUT MY PASTA DOUGH?

Using a wooden pin on a wooden board creates the best-textured pasta with a slightly roughened surface, making it ideal for sauce to cling to.

I DON'T HAVE A LONG PASTA ROLLING PIN. WHAT SHOULD I DO?

The answer to this question will depend on the pasta you want to make.

A long rolling pin, known as a mattarello, (90 cm/35 in or more) is used for egg pasta dough which is rolled into a sheet called a sfoglia.

If your rolling pin is about 30 cm (12 in) long and the dough uses 300 g (10½ oz/2½ cups) of flour, then you will have to cut the dough in thirds and roll three sfoglie. This is because the dough can be rolled into a sfoglia about 80 cm (31 in) in diameter, and using a small rolling pin will result in creases caused by its ends. The dough will also be uneven.

In other words, your rolling pin should always be longer than the diameter of the sfoglia you plan to roll out.

If you know you are going to roll out egg pasta regularly it's worth buying a good rolling pin – do a search on social media with the hashtag #mattarello. What is most important is: it shouldn't warp. A bowed rolling pin will give you uneven dough. So, make sure the maker uses seasoned wood.

If you are an occasional dabbler, then I suggest you go to your local hardware store or timber merchant and, along with the board

(see below), buy a wooden dowel or pole. They come in different diameters and can be cut to the length you want. Carla's rolling pin is a table leg, for example – see page 202.

These dowels are likely to end up warping, but they're cheap, so get another one and use the older one for hanging your tagliatelle; simply balance it between two chairs.

If you are rolling out semolina flour dough, normal-length rolling pins will be fine because one doesn't make ultra-thin pasta sheets with them.

DO I NEED A SPECIAL PASTA BOARD?

Yes. All our *signore* have dedicated pasta boards. This is because they don't want the dough picking up other flavours (e.g. onion) from the wood. Also, they only scrape and wipe down their board with a dry cloth to clean them. Wood magically wicks away moisture (silicone and plastic aren't great for working with pasta so avoid them). Unsealed marble is okay but it's not portable. You want a pasta board to be large; and even if you intend to buy rather than commission or make a board, do read the next section so you are aware of what to look for in a board.

HOW CAN I MAKE MY OWN PASTA BOARD?

I'm often asked this question! The ladies' boards tend to be ones made with whatever wood is available locally. This can be chestnut, cherry, beech, maple, birch, but not pine (too splintery) or olive (which twists eventually). You can spend a bit and commission an artisan-made one, or you can go to your local timber merchants who may be able to cut some solid wood for you; otherwise get some thick, not chemically treated, marine-grade birch plywood. You will need to add a lip under one long side to anchor it on the counter or table edge, and to stop it from slipping when you roll out the dough. Also, you will need to decide *where* you are going to use it, because this will determine its maximum size, and *how* you are going to use it, because a sfoglia egg pasta sheet will need more space than if you are only ever going to make cavatelli. Several nonne, in fact, use a wooden table or *madia*, a splendid design which looks like a deep chest of drawers, with a dough trough beneath the top that doubles as a pasta board.

Don't oil or seal the surface of your pasta board – just give it a light sanding.

IS IT OKAY TO USE A PASTA-ROLLING MACHINE?

Of course you can! Choose whatever method suits you. There is a difference in the texture of pasta rolled by machine rather than by hand – it's more slippery – but it depends on how much of a pasta obsessive you want to be. I personally think that by the time you've anchored the gadget to a suitable work surface, cut the dough into chunks, folded it each time before feeding it through the rollers and so on, it is just as quick – if not quicker – to roll it out with a pin. The stand alone electric motor ones are fun but are primarily for folk who make one heck of a lot of pasta.

WHAT ABOUT OTHER TOOLS?

- A spritzer water bottle is not essential, but helpful. It is useful when rolling shapes like maccheroni and the board can get a bit slippy; a mist of water helps to give a bit of a grip. You can also use it to moisten the pasta dough when sealing ravioli edges.
- Another useful tool is the bench scraper, which you use to mix the dough ingredients, or clean the board's surface. Our ladies often have cast-iron ones called a raschietto. They are no longer made, so you will have to scour Italian antique markets for one.

- A digital scale; think of it as L-plates while you practise becoming a fully-fledged sfoglina or sfoglino.
- A long straight-bladed knife for slicing pasta into ribbons.
- A grooved wooden gnocchi paddle, though the tines of a fork will do for gnocchi.
- If you want to make maccheroni, you will need a ferro, a metal rod, which apparently used to be made with umbrella spokes. Our ladies also use long grass stalks or ginestra twigs – in fact, anything thin, straight, with a bit of surface texture to stop the pasta from sticking works well: bamboo skewers, for example, or look for very thin wooden dowels.

WHAT IS 00 FLOUR?

Unfortunately, there isn't a globally recognised system of classification for flours for the home cook; every country does something different. In Italy, '00' refers to the ash residue of soft wheat flour. Scientists burn the flour and measure what minerals are left over; the higher the amount, the more bran is present. Thus, 00 has the least amount of ash, because most of the bran is removed. It is classified as having a 50% 'extraction rate'. The lack of bran makes 00 flour 'talcum powdery' which is why people say it's more finely ground; as you can see, it's a bit more complicated than that!

00 flour is usually combined with eggs, which gives the pasta a bit more body; you can add just water – and that's what folks did in the old days when eggs were sold for an income – but the pasta will be a bit soft. It is used mostly in central and northern Italian pasta dishes.

0 flour (the next grade) has a 72% extraction rate and this is approximately the same as all-purpose and plain flours in America and the UK.

It is more important to look at the protein content: your 00 flour should be between 9 and 11% protein. 0 flour should be between 11 and 12%. Check on the side of the flour packet for this information.

CAN I USE PLAIN OR ALL-PURPOSE FLOUR INSTEAD OF 00?

Yes, you can, but remember that non-Italian flour manufacturers use a mixture of soft and hard wheat varieties in their flours. Italian flour manufacturers only use soft wheat varieties; this soft/hard classification refers to how difficult it is to grind the grains into flour – and wheat varieties are not uniform. Thus, don't panic if you have to adjust the dough by adding more flour or water, and be prepared for the dough to behave a bit differently if you've used 00 previously.

WHAT IS SEMOLA RIMACINATA?

Semola is the Italian word for semolina, which is what is produced from milling the endosperm of durum wheat and it is used in the production of commercial pasta. Semola rimacinata is semolina which has been milled twice to give it a finer texture. I refer to this as 'semolina flour' in this book.

Durum wheat is a different species (Triticum durum) to ordinary wheat (Triticum aestivum) and its proteins are slightly different. When hydrated, they combine to give a gluten which is plastic (it holds its shape well when cooked) but not elastic (it's not very stretchy). It's difficult to make airy bread with it, for example, but it's great for pasta like cavatelli and maccheroni.

It is most often used in water-based pasta doughs from southern Italy.

CAN I USE BREAD OR STRONG FLOUR TO MAKE PASTA?

It's very unusual to use bread flour in pasta making, which is called *farina di Manitoba* in Italy. The high gluten levels (12–14%) make it a tough dough to roll. I have so far only come across one signora who uses it to make a type of corzetti – and the dough is not stretched or extended as you would when making a sfoglia.

WHAT ABOUT PASTA FLOUR?

If all the detail on 0 and 00 flours above sounds confusing, you can opt for 'pasta flour'. Some supermarkets have their own-brand versions, in addition to the flour manufacturers' product. They are a mixture of soft and durum wheat flours; they don't usually specify the ratios, but it's probably around 70:30. Cooks like Maria, on page 254, mix their own and she says this gives you the best of both types of flour: an extendable dough which is also a bit toothsome. It's a matter of personal taste to do this.

ARE SPECIALITY FLOURS SUITABLE FOR MAKING PASTA?

Heritage wheat, farro (emmer in America), spelt, barley, buckwheat and so on can all be used in pasta doughs. If you want to experiment, it's a good idea to start with small quantities mixed in with your usual flour as some, like buckwheat, contain no gluten which means the dough won't stick together if that's all you use. Gradually increase the amounts as you get used to the dough. Barley flour, for example, can be made into pasta but it's a very crumbly dough thanks to its low gluten levels and it takes lots of practise to master. You can 'cheat' by adding gluten powder, but that's for someone else to explain to you!

WHEN SHOULD I USE EGGS?

By and large, eggs are combined with 00 flour in pasta-making. The eggs should be the best quality you can afford; when there are only two ingredients the taste of each matters. In Italy, you can buy eggs especially for pasta making. The hens have been fed a diet rich in beta-carotene resulting in rich orange yolks, which makes the pasta look lovely. Lemon-yellow yolks, as long as they are good quality, will give a paler pasta that will taste the same.

The women we film don't bother to measure out their ingredients; their decades of experience mean they rely on touch and sight to make pasta, not a pair of scales. For the rest of us, however, they are quite useful! In Europe we use grams; I recommend measuring ingredients in grams because it's more accurate than cups and easier to calculate than ounces.

Broadly speaking there are two types of dough: egg pasta dough and durum wheat or semolina flour dough.

HOW DO I MAKE AN EGG PASTA DOUGH?

Our signore start with how many eggs they want to use, then determine the quantity of flour: one egg is used for every 100 g (3½ oz/ ⅔ cup) of flour for the rolling-pin method. In Italy, an egg without its shell weighs 55 g (2 oz); but eggs don't always weigh the same, and you may want to use other eggs like duck or turkey (like several of our nonne do), so in this book I also give you the grams of egg required for 55% hydration.

55 g (2 oz) beaten egg	100 g (3½ oz/⅔ cup) flour
110 g (3¾ oz) beaten egg	200 g (7 oz/1 ⅔ cups) flour
165 g (5¾ oz) beaten egg	300 g (10½ oz/2½ cups) flour
220 g (7¾ oz) beaten egg	400 g (14 oz/3 ⅓ cups) flour

If your total egg weight is just under 55 g (2 oz), top it up with water; or spoon a bit out if it's just over.

If you are using a pasta-rolling machine, your hydration should be very slightly less thanks to those metal rollers not wicking away moisture. Calculate for 50% hydration i.e. 50 g (1¾ oz) of egg for every 100 g (3½ oz/⅔ cup) of flour.

As a rule of thumb, allow 1 egg (55 g) and 100 g (3½ oz/⅔ cup) flour for every person; this is generous and will also depend on what you are dressing the pasta with.

To begin with, weigh out your eggs and flour separately. Tip the flour onto a pasta board and make a generous well in the middle in which to pour your eggs.

Crack the eggs into the well. Use a fork or your fingers to scramble them as if you are making an omelette; the liquid should not be clumpy with yolk and white but properly mixed together. Then, slowly draw in a bit of flour at a time, making sure there's a consistently smooth mixture with no flour-bergs. Eventually you'll end up with a bit of a shaggy mess which you should heap together; start working this dough into a ball. Use a light touch when the egg is still wet, so you do not get too much stuck to your hands.

When you have a ball of pasta dough and no flour left on the board, start kneading the dough. This is a soft massage where you use your body weight to lean in on the pasta and make a dent with the heel of your hand and push forward on the board. Flatten, push, then pull the pasta back over itself constantly for 10 minutes. Time it. You will end up with a smooth and bouncy ball of pasta.

Once it's kneaded, place the dough in a bowl that fits the size of your ball and cover it with a close-fitting lid or dampened cloth which has not been cleaned in perfumed detergent; air is the enemy of pasta, and you don't want it to dry out. Let this rest for at least 30 minutes, 45–60 minutes is even better, so it will relax enough to roll easily. If you leave it overnight in the fridge, the dough might discolour a bit, but it will taste the same. Remember to bring it to room temperature before rolling it out.

First of all: channel your favourite Pasta Granny. Watch her video several times.

Once your dough has rested, and it's a nice round ball, pat it down into a disc on your pasta board and take your pin in both hands.

Roll out the dough, turning it the same direction a few degrees every time. When the dough is the size of a large plate, start rolling the outer third of the circle, and keep turning the dough through 90 degrees in the same direction. Stop your pin just before the edge of the dough so it doesn't get all ragged and thin around the circumference. Every 6 or 7 strokes, roll the pasta up around the pin, give it a tug, so it's a good fit and not baggy, then roll it out to iron out the central 'bump' in the dough.

Everyone finds their own method for rolling; I use a 'breaststroke swimming' technique: start with your hands in the middle of the pin, then push and smooth your hands over the top of the pin to its edges. Bring them to the centre again as you pull the pin back.

Your sfoglia will eventually become too big to turn by hand, so roll it up over your pin, smoothing the pasta as you do so, before turning it, and rolling it out again, using the same smoothing, swimming method.

You can drape the sfoglia off the edge of your board to help anchor and stretch it. Be careful not to lean against it, though.

If your dough hydration is correct you won't need tons of flour on your board or the pasta. It shouldn't crack, it shouldn't stick to your pin; it should feel and drape like heavy linen.

If it's a very dry day, cover the dough with a damp tea towel (ensure you use one that has been laundered without perfumed detergent) while you work, for example, on a row of ravioli.

To check your sfoglia is evenly rolled out (the reason you need to do this is so the pasta cooks evenly) roll up about a third over your pin – keeping hold of the edges – then hold it up to the light. Darker patches mean thicker dough so lay it back out and go over these areas again.

Leave your pasta sheet to dry on the board for 10–15 minutes. For tagliolini, tagliatelle and pappardelle, lightly dust it with flour, roll it up very gently as you would a carpet and it's now ready for cutting.

Durum wheat flour only needs water adding to it; that said, some of our ladies add an egg to the dough, by way of being generous to their guests, not out of necessity. As I've already mentioned, it's great for making shapes, though of course it's also good for tagliatelle and so on; the ribbons won't be quite as thin as you can achieve with a 00-based dough.

You want 45–50% hydration for this dough, or 45–50 g (1½ –1¾ oz) of water for every 100 g (3½ oz/⅔ cup) of flour. Some cooks like to add salt, not for flavour but to help the gluten strands slide over one another. Allow 4 g (1 teaspoon) salt for every litre of water – simply stir and dissolve.

Sift the semolina flour into a large bowl and pour the 45% dose of water into the flour. Work the dough with strong hands – no need to be gentle here – to gather it into a ball for kneading. Use the extra 15 ml (1 tablespoon) of water only if you really can't get the dough to form after trying for a good minute or two. Semola has a tendency to trick novices into thinking you need more hydration than necessary, as it feels dry until you have worked it for a bit.

When you have formed a ball, turn it out onto the pasta board and knead for 5 minutes until smooth and lightly bouncy. If you would like to start forming your pasta right away there is no need to let it rest as you do with 00 flour dough. Otherwise, cover it until you are ready.

If you do end up doing a long knead (for whatever reason, too busy chatting with pals? Losing yourself in a podcast?) the gluten gets uptight and then you do have to let it rest for 30 minutes. After resting, follow the instructions in the recipe.

HELP! I DON'T HAVE TIME TO MAKE PASTA, WHAT SHOULD I DO?

Fear not, the pasta police will not come knocking at your door. You can swap most of the pasta shapes in this book with dried pasta alternatives, and I've added suggestions where applicable.

Remember, dried pasta is always made with semolina flour, so if you're swapping it in an egg pasta recipe it will have a different mouthfeel. Maybe you'll be too hungry to notice, and that's fine. Dried pasta is not necessarily an inferior product to fresh pasta – the key is to find good-quality dried pasta, and price is a good indicator (unless the packaging is very fancy). Look for the words 'extruded through bronze dies' and 'dried at low temperatures'. My friend Lorenzo Settimi at Pasta Mancini always says when you open a bag of pasta, sniff it; if it's good quality you'll be able to smell the wheat.

WHAT'S THE BEST WAY TO COOK PASTA?

I think the 'use huge pots to cook pasta' recommendations come from chefs in restaurant kitchens, because the ladies I film always manage to produce lovely pasta from smallish pans: it takes ages and costs money to heat up a large pan of water. Just use a sensible saucepan; if you are cooking for a party, boil the pasta in batches if necessary, scooping the cooked pasta out and adding to the *condimento* or dressing.

It doesn't make any difference whether you add the salt to cold water or to boiling, though with the latter you must ensure the water returns to the boil before adding your pasta. Use non-iodized, coarse sea salt. Allow about 10 g (½ oz) per litre – it should be a bit saltier than you think.

You do not need to add oil – it's an expensive ingredient, and an extravagance to pour it down the sink. And it doesn't stop pasta from sticking! Stir the pasta gently while it cooks instead.

HOW DO YOU KNOW WHEN IT'S DONE?

Nibble a piece; how long it takes to cook will depend on the size you've made your pasta shapes and how freshly made they are. Once the water has returned to the boil, allow a minute for ribbon pasta like tagliatelle (less if it's extra-thin like tagliolini), and 3–5 minutes for filled pasta.

For semolina pasta, expect to cook it for at least 5 minutes. The more dried out the pasta is, the longer it will take to cook.

Some cooks like to add a little of the pasta cooking water to make the finished dish creamier. This is a matter of judgement about the thickness of your sauce; it's not routine for the Pasta Grannies.

Andiamo in cucina!

CHEESE

Most of the recipes in this book call for a *formaggio grana* (hard cheese) to be grated over the dish at the end of cooking. In the north of Italy this is often Parmigiano Reggiano, and the cheese should be aged for at least 18 months. The older it is, the more granular, more savoury and more expensive it becomes.

As general guidance: 12–18-month aged Parmigiano is good for shaving over salads; 24-month-aged Parmigiano is good for cooking; and older than 36 months is best when savoured at the beginning or end of a meal. It's a bit extravagant to use in cooking!

Grana Padano is an alternative cheese. It tends to be a bit cheaper, as the process by which it's made isn't the same as the process for Parmigiano (it matures more quickly thanks to a lower fat content, for example). For my taste buds I find it can lack the complexity of Parmigiano, but you can find some outstanding examples of Grana Padano. As with all cheeses, try and find out a bit about the producer, and taste it before buying (this is not always possible, I know).

Sheep's cheese, pecorino, is found all over central and southern Italy. There are lots of different kinds – some of which are famous, like Pecorino Romano and Pecorino Sardo. If you cannot get hold of them, use an artisan-made hard sheep's milk cheese local to you.

Ricotta can be made with sheep, cow or goat's milk. Sheep and goat's ricotta have a great flavour but they are also more prone to hanging on to their whey; you'll need to drain the ricotta in a sieve for 60 minutes or so. You can also find versions with added cream (called fiocca in my local supermarket) in the north, while in the south it is salted and aged to produce ricotta salata. Another way of preserving ricotta is to smoke it; this is grated over pasta at the end.

FATS

The ubiquity and popularity of olive oil has only come about since the Second World War. Traditionally, in central and northern Italy, pork fat was used in cooking as *strutto* (lard). In the north of Italy, butter is used – one can even buy it in kilo (2 lb 4 oz) blocks. I have come to the conclusion from filming over 300 women, it's not the fat that's important for a healthy long life – it is the moderation with which it is consumed, and the active lifestyle signore have lived.

Olive oil is the fat listed in most of the recipes in this book; by this I mean extra-virgin olive oil. What is more important than its nationality is its freshness. Buy it in tins or dark bottles so it keeps better and check its date of processing – don't buy it if it is over a year old. And don't save it for special occasions!

FISH

Always try and buy fresh fish, because frozen fish will release a lot of water (30-50%) during cooking, resulting in smaller portion size and a drier texture. Never cook it with a rolling boil or over a high heat; a low simmer is all that's needed.

HERBS

Use fresh herbs! You'll never see dried in an Italian kitchen, with the exception of oregano in the south (this is in fact the dried flowers, which you can either buy ready crumbled or as bunches).

Use a very sharp knife for cutting so you don't bruise the leaves. And remember, Italians use flat-leaf parsley, not the curly kind.

TOMATOES

Bottling and preserving tomatoes is still
a widespread summer activity for families
in Italy. Folks either grow their own, or order
in bulk from a friendly farmer. The tomatoes
are sieved before bottling and the resulting
sauce is called passata. The next best thing
to do, if preserving your own isn't possible,
is to buy tins of good quality, whole tomatoes
called *pomodori pelati* (peeled tomatoes) and
blitz them with a stick blender. None of our
Grannies I've filmed has used pre-chopped
toms, or *polpa di pomodoro*.

CONCENTRATO DI POMODORO

In the industrial process, pulped and sieved
tomatoes are placed in special evaporating
machines to drive off their moisture. There
are two grades, *concentrato* and the thicker
doppio concentrato, where 5–6 kg (11–13 lb)
of tomatoes are needed to make 1 kg (2 lb 2 oz)
of paste. In Sicily, the domestically-made paste
is called *estratto* in Italian, or *strattu* in Sicilian.
Of course, home preservers don't measure
concentration, but their paste is even thicker
than the version you buy in tins or tubes. If you
ever visit Sicily, try and buy some to take home
with you as it's much more savoury and delicious.

one

herbs,
nuts
&
spices

ADELE'S GATTAFIN

♦♦♦

FRIED RAVIOLI FROM LEVANTO

PREP	1 hour
SERVINGS	40 pieces

FOR THE PASTA

300 g (10½ oz/2½ cups) 00 flour
2 g (½ teaspoon) salt
50 ml (1¾ fl oz/3½ tablespoons)
  extra-virgin olive oil
50 ml (1¾ fl oz/3½ tablespoons)
  dry white wine
50 ml (1¾ fl oz/3½ tablespoons)
  warm water

FOR THE FILLING AND FRYING

1 kg (2 lb 4 oz) mixed greens
  with tough stalks removed
  (trimmed weight)
500 g (1 lb 2 oz) red onions,
  finely diced
4 tablespoons extra-virgin olive oil
nutmeg, to taste
1 egg, beaten
50 g (1¾ oz) 24 month old
  Parmigiano Reggiano, grated
25 g (1 oz) Pecorino Sardo, grated
1 tablespoon chopped
  flat-leaf parsley
1 teaspoon roughly chopped
  marjoram
handful of dry breadcrumbs
  (if necessary)
neutral oil, for frying
salt

What is more delicious than ravioli? Fried ravioli! And Adele's gattafin recipe is definitely one you should try. They are a speciality of Levanto, a village close to the Cinque Terre national park in Liguria. When we first visited Adele, we said, 'Please don't worry, we only need to film enough for a plateful.' Adele replied with a knowing smile, 'Well, I've made extra anyway because you must try them and one is never enough.' She was right.

Ideally, these should be made with foraged greens which give the dish a more complex, deeper flavour; Adele's harvest included dandelions, sow thistles, wild fennel, poppy, borage, rocket and wild chard. However, they'll still be delicious if all you can find in your supermarket is spinach, rocket and some not-too-bitter radicchio.

Make the pasta dough as described on page 11, but instead of using eggs, add the salt, olive oil, white wine and water. Form a dough and knead it for 10 minutes, then leave it to rest, covered, for 30 minutes. Incidentally, Adele says this dough makes excellent tagliatelle; she is particularly fond of serving it with a game-bird ragù.

While the pasta rests, prepare the greens for the filling. Wash the trimmed leaves in plenty of cold water; this is especially important if you've collected them from your garden or the countryside.

Bring a pan of salted water to the boil and add the greens. Cook the leaves until they are collapsed and tender– how long this takes will depend on your selection.

Heat the olive oil in a frying pan over a medium heat, then add the onions and sauté with a pinch of salt for 7–10 minutes until soft. Don't let them go brown.

Add the greens to the onions and fry the mixture for several more minutes until it starts to dry out but remains moist enough to squish together and form into balls. Season the mixture generously with salt and some nutmeg and leave it to cool in a bowl.

When it is cold enough to work with your hands, add the egg, both cheeses, the parsley and the marjoram. Squish everything together. If the filling feels wet and sloppy, add a handful of breadcrumbs and let the filling sit for 10 minutes to allow the breadcrumbs to absorb the moisture.

Roll out the pasta dough to a thickness of 1 mm. If this is a bit tricky for you to achieve by hand, then a pasta machine is fine.

Recipe continued next page →

Recipe continued →

Use a 10 cm (4 in) pastry cutter or upside down glass to cut out pasta discs by pressing firmly through the dough – you will end up with about 40 discs. Try and do this in an orderly fashion so the circles are all close together; that way you don't waste dough. Scoop a walnut-sized portion of filling and place it on the top half of each pasta disc. You're going to fold the bottom half over the top, but first use a spray bottle of water and finely mist each pasta round, holding the bottle at least a 30 cm (12 in) above it so the dough won't become too wet. This will help the dough to seal well; its oil content can hinder it from being sticky.

Fold the half of pasta which doesn't have filling over the top to form a half moon shape. Pinch and press the edges together really well. Pat each gattafin gently to flatten it slightly – this helps to flip them when you are frying them.

Take a deep-sided sauté pan and pour in neutral oil to a depth of about 5 cm (2 in). Heat it to 180°C/350°F. Adele uses a wooden skewer to test the temperature of the oil: she dips it into the oil and when bubbles form around the wood, the oil is hot enough. Fry just a few gattafin at a time – there needs to enough space and plenty of oil around them for even cooking. The gattafin cook quickly, so flip them frequently until they are lovely and golden (this will take 2–3 minutes). Use a spider to scoop them out and plonk them on kitchen paper or brown paper to drain the excess oil.

Sprinkle them with salt and watch them disappear as fast as you can make them.

BIANCA'S LASAGNA AL PESTO

◆◆◆

BASIL PESTO LASAGNA FROM LIGURIA

PREP	1½ hours
SERVINGS	6

DRIED PASTA ALTERNATIVE	Lasagna sheets

Bianca lives in Boccadasse, a picturesque village and harbour which is now part of Genova; it continues to have an active small fishing fleet, and is hugely popular with locals and visitors who throng the harbour bars. Bianca and her family own the local butchers, although she is retired and her son runs the business. She now has the time to cook for her grandsons, Leonardo and Pietro, who live in the apartment above hers.

Bianca first learned to cook as a young girl. Her mother had received electric shock therapy for depression and was told that having another child would help her; so, Bianca arrived several years after her siblings and as she grew up it became her job to cook for her family. But Bianca's real talent is calligraphy. When she was 14, she got herself a job writing the tax discs for a local car club because her writing was so good. And it was only when she met her butcher husband that she changed jobs.

It's worth making this lasagna from scratch. Fresh shop-bought lasagna sheets have semolina flour in them, and they result in a thicker, firmer layer of pasta. Bianca likes to buy her basil as rooted plants wrapped in newspaper; they are a common sight in the vegetable markets of Liguria. And please make sure your pine nuts are from Italy – it will say so on the packet and they will be more expensive. They should be from the pine tree Pinus pinea, not other pine species.

FOR THE PASTA
300 g (10½ oz/2½ cups) 00 flour
165 g (5¾ oz) egg or 3 eggs

FOR THE PESTO
120 g (4¼ oz) fresh basil leaves
3 fresh garlic cloves, crushed
30 g (1 oz) Italian pine nuts, lightly toasted
100 ml (3½ fl oz/scant ½ cup) extra-virgin olive oil, plus extra if necessary
50 g (1¾ oz) grated Parmigiano Reggiano (preferably aged for 24 months), plus a handful extra for the topping
10 g (½ oz) grated Pecorino Sardo
fine sea salt

Make the pasta dough as described on page 11.

Roll out the pasta dough to a thickness of 1 mm – the thinner the pasta, the more layers you'll be able to squeeze in! Cut your dough sheet into pieces to fit the shape and size of a 30 x 20 x 8 cm (12 x 8 x 3 in) baking/lasagna dish – you should have about 5 layers. Place them on a tablecloth or kitchen paper.

If you have a pestle and mortar, use it to make the pesto as described on page 36; if not, place the basil, garlic and pine nuts in a food processor and pulse them until roughly chopped, then pour in the olive oil and keep pulsing it until the pesto is creamy but not entirely smooth. Scrape the pesto into a bowl, stir through the grated cheeses and adjust the seasoning with salt – it may not need any. Add more pecorino cheese if you want more zing.

FOR THE BÉCHAMEL

70 g (2½ oz) unsalted butter
70 g (2½ oz) 0 flour
500 ml (17 fl oz/generous 2 cups)
    cold full-fat (whole) milk
freshly grated nutmeg, to taste
salt

FOR THE VEGETABLES

1 large potato, peeled and cut into
    1 cm (½ in)-thick slices
150 g (5 oz) trimmed green beans,
    halved

Now, make the béchamel. Melt the butter in a deep pan over a medium heat, then add the flour. Start whisking the two together until a blond roux forms. Cook it for a minute or so, then pour in the cold milk all at once and keep whisking the mixture well until you have a thickened sauce. Season it with salt and nutmeg. Do this step just before you are ready to assemble the lasagna – you don't want a skin forming on the béchamel.

Preheat the oven to 165°C/325°F (gas 3).

Fill a mixing bowl with cold water. Spread a few tea towels or a tablecloth (laundered using perfume-free detergent) on a work surface. Bring a saucepan of salted water to the boil and blanch the pasta sheets a couple at a time for 1 minute, stirring them to stop them sticking, then plop them in the cold water for a couple of minutes before spreading them out on the tea towels to dry. Lastly, boil the potato slices and beans together for 4 minutes in the pasta water. Scoop them out and have them ready for assembly.

Spread a layer of béchamel over the base of the 30 x 20 x 8 cm (12 x 8 x 3 in) baking/lasagna dish, then mix in a tablespoon of the pesto. Add a layer of pasta, then repeat with more béchamel sauce and pesto to make at least 5 layers.

Dress the potatoes and green beans with the leftover pesto and béchamel and spread them evenly on top of your last layer. Finish with a generous sprinkle of grated Parmigiano Reggiano and bake the lasagna in the oven for about 40 minutes. Turn on the top grill and grill for the last 5 minutes to give the dish a browned crust if this hasn't happened already.

Remove the lasagna from the oven and let it sit for 10 minutes before serving to hungry children.

CICCI'S TAGLIERINI CON PORCINI

◆◆◆

NETTLE TAGLIOLINI WITH PORCINI SAUCE FROM LIGURIA

PREP	1 hour, plus resting time
SERVINGS	5–6

'If my parents could see our woodlands now, they'd be heartbroken. They're a mess! Now no-one cares for them because no one lives here anymore!' Cicci lives alone in a hamlet a 20-minute drive from the nearest village in the Apennine mountains of Liguria. 'In the old days we would prune the trees and clear the undergrowth and this vegetation would be given to the cows for their stalls.' Cicci heaved a sigh, 'It was easy to find porcini then, now I really have to look for them.'

Apart from a few years when her two children were at school and the family had to move to the nearby town of Gattorna, Cicci has lived here all her life. The road only reached her *borgo* (village) when she was 20 years old. The remoteness doesn't bother her. 'Actually,' she whispered, so her daughter Laura couldn't hear, 'sometimes I take the phone off the hook so people cannot bother me.' She doesn't have a mobile phone because there is no signal.

Back in the day, Cicci wasn't alone; the countryside was really quite busy, with several hamlets scattered through the woodlands. Cicci's husband Giorgio grew up 3 kilometres away and they had known each other since they were kids, before getting engaged when she was 18 years old. Giorgio was a woodcutter, selling logs to folks down in the valley, while Cicci's family were dairy farmers. 'Without the road it was difficult to sell cheeses and sometimes they went bad. Nobody had much money, but neighbours helped each other with whatever needed to be done.'

Tasks included clearing meadows in the forests to grow hay for the cattle and maintaining the terraces on which families grew vegetables and crops; essentials like potatoes, pulses, tomatoes, wheat and maize. In autumn, people gathered chestnuts from which they made flour, and hunted wild boar for making sausages.

Looking after cows meant Cicci used butter in her cooking and, like Pina on page 42, she is fond of adding a little cream to her pesto. The best time to forage nettles for her tagliarini (the local name for tagliolini) is spring, when the leaves are young, and thanks to modern gadgetry like a freezer, she can freeze both her nettles and porcini for year-round use. Nettles can, of course, be swapped for something more readily available such as spinach or Swiss chard. Use ordinary button mushrooms if fresh porcini are too expensive or impossible to find.

Recipe continued next page →

FOR THE NETTLE PASTA

300 g (10½ oz) foraged nettles
160 g (5½ oz) egg
1 teaspoon chopped marjoram
20 ml (¾ fl oz) white wine
400 g (14 oz/3⅓ cups) 00 flour

FOR THE PORCINI SAUCE

20 g (¾ oz) dried porcini
100 g (3½ oz) onion
1 tablespoon finely chopped
    flat-leaf parsley
100 ml (3½ fl oz/scant ½ cup)
    extra-virgin olive oil
    (or a good slice of butter)
300 g (10½ oz) fresh or frozen
    porcini (or other mushrooms)
½ tablespoon tomato paste
400 g (14 oz) passata
200 ml (7 fl oz/scant 1 cup) porcini
    soaking water, strained
1 fresh bay leaf or 2 dried ones
salt and pepper

First, prepare the nettles for the pasta dough.

Use gloves to handle the nettles (as if you need reminding!). Rinse and clean the nettles in a sink of cold water then dump them in a pan of boiling unsalted water and cook the leaves for about 5 minutes until tender. Place a sieve in the sink and drain the nettles then run cold water through them to make them easier to handle. Once cooked, they lose their sting, so you can use your hands to squeeze out as much water as possible.

Straggly bits of leaf don't make a good dough, so either use a food mill, like Cicci does, or a food processor, to mince or chop the leaves into a thick puree. Weigh it; you want 40 g (1½ oz) puree.

In a bowl, mix this nettle mush with the egg, marjoram and wine. Make a flour well on your board and pour the nettle and egg mixture into the centre, then use a fork or your fingers to mix the wet and dry ingredients together. Using your hands, smoosh it all together to make a uniform ball of dough. Knead this for 10 minutes as described on page 11.

Rest the dough, covered, for a good 30 minutes.

Roll out the pasta dough to a thickness of 1 mm. Cicci uses a pasta-rolling machine to roll it out to a 20 cm (8 in)-long sheet and cut the tagliarini – this certainly makes for uniform pasta. Otherwise, you can use a long rolling pin (*mattarello*) to make a 1 mm-thick dough sheet (sfoglia). Roll it up loosely like a carpet and cut it into very thin ribbons. Toss the strands loose and let them dry on your board for 30–60 minutes before cooking. Doing this will help the tagliarini keep their bite when they are cooked.

For the porcini sauce, clean the dried porcini mushrooms with a brush to remove any possible dirt, then rinse them quickly in cold water. Place the mushrooms in a heatproof bowl, cover them with 200 ml (7 fl oz/scant 1 cup) warm water and leave them to rehydrate for 20 minutes by which time the water will be brown. Remove the mushrooms and reserve the soaking water.

Depending on your choice of gadgetry, blitz or mince the onion and parsley together.

Heat the olive oil (or butter) in a saucepan over a low heat, add the onion puree and soften for 5 minutes.

Next, blitz or mince the rehydrated porcini; if you are using a food mill, use a plate with slightly larger holes. Add this rough puree to the softened onion; you'll need to stir it frequently as the porcini tends to stick to the bottom of the pan.

If you are using fresh porcini, lucky you; wipe them with a damp cloth or soft brush to rid them of dirt. Cut the fresh or frozen porcini into 2 cm (¾ in) chunks and add them to the mix, followed by the tomato paste and passata.

Strain the soaked mushroom water through a fine-mesh sieve into the vegetable mixture. Season with salt and add

the bay leaves and simmer for 20 minutes. Don't feel tempted to leave it for ages if you are using fresh porcini, as they will turn to mush.

Bring a large saucepan of salted water to the boil. Tip in the tagliarini and give the contents a good stir to stop the ribbons from sticking together. They won't take long to cook; start test-nibbling a piece after a minute or so. Once cooked, drain them thoroughly.

Warm a capacious pasta bowl or platter.

Spoon some sauce over the base, then tip the pasta onto it, followed by the rest of the sauce. Toss everything together and distribute it in smaller bowls to your hungry guests.

This dish doesn't need cheese, but of course you can add some grated Pecorino if you fancy it. Freshly ground black pepper will bring out the porcini flavour.

HERBS, NUTS & SPICES

IDA'S CHOCOLATE BUNET

◆◆◆

CHOCOLATE PUDDING FROM PIEDMONT

Bunet is a classic dessert from Piedmont and every home cook has her version of it. This is 93-year-old Ida's recipe, or rather her mother-in-law's recipe because Ida learnt it from her. She likes to serve it for Christmas, and it's an ideal sweet to have up your sleeve for the holidays, as it's simple to make. Ida is one of our 'star grannies', women we return to to film whenever possible, and she features in the first Pasta Grannies book too where she shares stories of her life.

Traditionally this is a brick shape, but you can of course experiment and serve individual portions.

PREP	1½ hours, plus cooling
SERVINGS	12

FOR THE CARAMEL

100 g (3½ oz/½ cup)
   caster (superfine) sugar
100 ml (3½ fl oz/scant ½ cup) water

FOR THE CUSTARD

100 g (3½ oz) Amaretti cookies
100 g (3½ oz) toasted hazelnuts
100 g (3½ oz) dark chocolate, grated
50 g (1¾ oz) unsweetened
   cocoa powder
1 litre (34 fl oz/4¼ cups)
   full-fat milk
8 eggs
120 g (4¼ oz/generous ½ cup)
   caster (superfine) sugar
1 tablespoon rum
1 tablespoon vanilla extract

Mix the water with the sugar in a non-stick saucepan, place it over a medium heat and, once it starts simmering, reduce the heat and – without ever stirring it – cook the caramel for about 10 minutes until it is a honey coloured. Carefully pour the caramel into a 30 x 13 x 8 cm (12 x 5 x 3 in) loaf tin and try to line the bottom and sides evenly (one of those silicone brushes can be helpful here). Let the tin cool down while you prepare the custard mix.

Preheat the oven to 180°C (350°F/gas 4).

The custard needs to cook in a bain marie, so half-fill a large roasting tin with water. Place the tin in the oven while mixing the custard ingredients.

Use a food processor to blitz the Amaretti cookies and toasted hazelnuts to a coarse crumb, then add the dark chocolate and the cocoa powder and pulse it until becomes powdery. Be cautious about this – overdo it and the chocolate will melt.

Warm the milk until you cannot stick your finger in it, but it's not boiling.

Beat the eggs with the sugar in a large bowl, then add the warm milk, rum and vanilla extract. Stir through the dry ingredients then transfer the about-to-be custard into the caramel-lined tin. Remove the roasting tin from the oven, place the loaf tin in the middle and return it to the oven.

Bake for 45–60 minutes until set. Start testing it with a wooden skewer after 45 minutes; it should come out clean when you stick it into the middle of the custard.

Remove the loaf tin from the oven, take it out of the water, and let it cool before un-moulding it onto a platter. First, release the sides by gently running a table knife along the edges of the tin, then reheat its bottom by placing the tin in a small amount of hot water for about 45 seconds. Pat the base dry. Place the platter over the tin and flip it, while making sure you clamp the plate and tin together. Be decisive; gravity will ensure the bunet escapes the tin.

Serve in thick slices.

NADIA'S MANDILLI DI SAEA CON PESTO

◆◆◆

SILK HANDKERCHIEFS WITH BASIL PESTO FROM LIGURIA

PREP	45 minutes
SERVES	4–6

Mandilli di saea translates as silk handkerchiefs; these large pasta squares should be very thin and light. And our Pasta Granny who shared her recipe with us is artist Nadia, who lives in the mountains of Liguria near Lumarzo. She is keen on living in harmony with nature; she won't even disturb spiders' cobwebs because she says 'they have a job to do'. And she is in the right spot to enjoy her surroundings: from her kitchen-sink window she looks out at the edge of a forest and regularly sees deer and the occasional wolf.

She loves growing her own vegetables and cooking from scratch. She even makes her own flour using locally grown whole wheat; it has a wonderful nutty aroma, but don't worry, you do not need to do this! We tested her recipe using 00 flour. If you do want to copy Nadia and use your own wholewheat flour, then sift the flour first, to remove the flakes of bran, otherwise your silk handkerchiefs will be more hessian in texture.

FOR THE PASTA

400 g (14 oz/3⅓ cups) 00 flour
220 g (7¾ oz) egg or 4 large eggs

FOR THE PESTO

1 garlic clove
70 g (2½ oz) Italian pine nuts, raw or lightly toasted
60 g (2 oz) Genovese basil leaves
120 ml (4 fl oz/½ cup) extra-virgin olive oil (ideally soft, grassy-flavoured Ligurian oil)
50 g (1¾ oz) Parmigiano Reggiano, grated
50 g (1¾ oz) Pecorino Sardo, grated
fine sea salt, to taste

Make the egg pasta dough as described on page 11, then leave it to rest, covered, for a good 30 minutes.

Roll out the dough as thinly as possible; you should be able to read through it! This equates to 0.5 mm thickness. You can use a pasta machine if you think you won't be able to manage this.

Dust flour over the pasta sheet then roll it up around your rolling pin, take a knife and slice lengthways through all the layers. The pasta will fall from the pin in rectangular strips which are magically the same width. Pile the strips one on top of the other and slice them horizontally to create squares. The exact size will depend slightly on the thickness of your rolling pin, but they should be about 15 cm (6 in) squares. Well done if they remind you of silk hankies!

To make the pesto, remove the skin from the garlic clove and halve the clove lengthways. If there's a green shoot (or *anima*, as Italians call it), hoik it out and discard.

Put the clove in a mortar with the pine nuts, then pound with the pestle and grind the two together into a rough paste.

Wash and dry the basil leaves thoroughly. Add a handful at a time to the mortar, with a pinch of salt, then pound and grind the leaves into the paste.

Stir through the grated cheeses and loosen the mixture with some of the extra-virgin olive oil; you may not need all of it. You now have a thick but stirrable pesto. If you want to use a stick blender or food processor, the result will be smoother and the flavour very slightly different, but not significant enough to cause face-pulling at the table.

Recipe continued next page → **HERBS, NUTS & SPICES**

Bring a large pan of salted water to the boil. Add the pasta squares, give them a stir and return the water to the boil. They should take about a minute to cook once they've returned to the boil, but test one to see. Scoop a cup of water out of the pan before draining the pasta. Return the squares to the pan and stir through the pesto, adding a little of the reserved cooking water to make it more saucy if necessary.

Serve on a beautiful platter with more grated cheese if you feel like it.

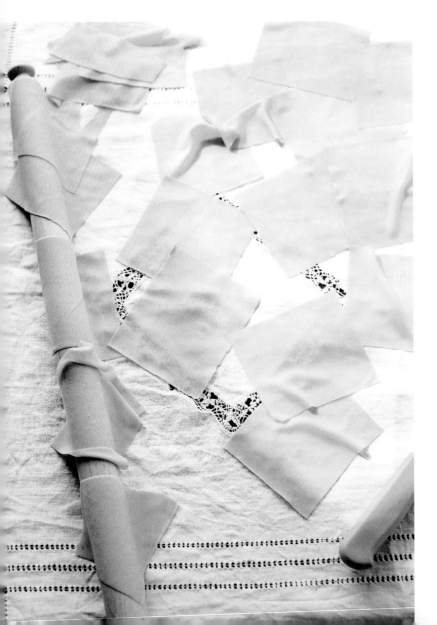

NORMA'S CVERCIA O MERVICE

❖❖❖

CRUMBLED LOVAGE 'PANCAKES' FROM FRIULI VENEZIA GIULIA

PREP	15–20 minutes
SERVINGS	4

40–50 g (1½–1¾ oz) lovage
30 g (1 oz) fresh chamomile
200 g (7 oz/1 ⅔ cups) 0 flour
100 ml (3½ fl oz/scant ½ cup) full-fat milk
6 eggs
12 g (½ oz) salt

FOR COOKING
4 tablespoons olive oil

Norma lived in Canada for 40 years, running a cleaning business with her husband. When he passed away, she returned to her home near Udine in Friuli Venezia Giulia. She lives high in the hills, which straddle the Italian border with Slovenia. 'I'm not leaving! There are only three people in the village who live here full time, but I love it.'

Cvercia is a pancake batter which is then scrambled rather than allowed to set. It has several names; elsewhere in the valley it's called *mervice*, and the translation into Italian is *briciole* which means 'crumbs'. It was traditionally a farm labourer's breakfast. It's quick to make, fills you up and is good with eggs should you have them.

These days, lovage isn't associated with Italian cooking, but the Ancient Romans were very fond it; the herb was used in the making of garum, the fermented fish condiment beloved in those times. It has a curry-celery flavour. Lovage is excellent in soups and salads and it's easy to grow; one plant will be enough for most cooks' needs. If you cannot get hold of it, swap it with celery leaves and ½ a teaspoon of freshly ground cumin seeds, or a pinch of mild curry powder. For the chamomile, soak a good-quality teabag for a minute or so and use the leaves. Neighbours of Norma like to use a mixture of mint and dill or fennel instead of the lovage and chamomile.

Chop the herbs together, as you would parsley. Scrape them into a bowl and add the flour, milk, eggs and salt. Use a stick blender or whisk to blitz or mix everything together. Norma made this as one big serving, but I found it's easier to scramble smaller quantities. So, in a small pan, over a gentle heat, melt the butter with the oil. Leave a non-stick frying pan over a medium heat on the adjacent burner on your hob for several minutes until hot. Pour a third of the oil-and-butter mix over the base of the frying pan. Add roughly a third of the batter and use a spatula to stir it about briskly for 3–5 minutes until you have green lumps. Taste one – the flour should be cooked through. Scrape the batch onto a warmed platter and repeat with the rest of the oil-and-butter mix and batter. This tastes even better after a couple of minutes.

PINA'S GNOCCHI DI CASTAGNE CON PESTO

◆◆◆

CHESTNUT GNOCCHI WITH WALNUT PESTO FROM LIGURIA

PREP 2 hours
SERVINGS 4–6

FOR THE GNOCCHI

500 g (1 lb 2 oz) floury potatoes
150 g (5 oz/1¼ cups) 00 flour plus
    an extra 35–40 g (1–1½ oz)
    for the board
50 g (1¾ oz/⅓ cup)
    chestnut flour
5 g (1 teaspoon) salt
freshly ground pepper, to serve

FOR THE PESTO

1 garlic clove
100 g (3½ oz) walnuts
100 ml (3½ fl oz/scant ½ cup)
    extra-virgin olive oil
30 g (1 oz) basil
50 g (1¾ oz) Parmigiano
    Reggiano, grated
50 g (1¾ oz) thick cream

'I don't understand why you come all the way up here to film me make gnocchi; can't you make them yourselves?' 91-year-old Pina thought we were mad not to have this life skill. Like Cicci (on page 29), Pina lives in the mountains behind Genova in Liguria, though they live about 2 hours' drive from each other. Pina ran the village bakery and shop for many years, and still has a few shelves with emergency packets of pasta and tinned tomatoes for when her neighbours get caught short. She used to carry the provisions on her back for the last two kilometres before the road got built, and even now only three-wheeled scooters can navigate the village's cobbled paths.

Making the most of what you have is second nature to Pina: she uses walnuts because pine nuts are too expensive, she grows her own potatoes, and the foraged chestnuts make more costly wheat flour go further. So, in that spirit, if you don't have chestnut flour, make these using just wheat flour.

First, make the gnocchi. Pina boils her potatoes with the skin on; an alternative is to bake the potatoes in a moderate oven as this gives them a nice fluffy texture. Whichever method you choose, once the spuds are soft, remove the skins and mash the flesh. Have your extra flour for the board to hand and don't leave the mash to cool: dump it straight onto your wooden board while it's still steaming, using a spoon. This moisture helps you to make a good dough. Mix the flours and salt and mush the mixture into the mash, then gently knead the mixture until you obtain a smooth non-sticky dough that does not break apart. Stop as soon as you get to this point; you don't want to overwork the dough.

Use some of the extra flour to dust your board and roll out ropes of dough about 2 cm (¾ in) in diameter and then cut each rope into two-finger-wide pieces. Use the same two fingertips to press into each gnocco and pull it back gently across the board to flatten and curl the dough. The results are gnocchi which look like thick or rustic cavatelli. Keep them well floured and spread out.

For the pesto, put the garlic, walnuts and oil into the bowl of a food processor and blitz until you have a rough paste. Now add the basil and blend again, before adding the Parmigiano. You want a thick, smooth sauce. Use a spatula to scrap the pesto into a bowl and stir through the cream.

Bring a large saucepan of heavily salted water to the boil. Tip in the gnocchi and give them a good stir to stop them from sticking. Once the water has returned to the boil, try the gnocchi every 30 seconds or so to see if they are cooked. When they are done, drain them through a colander.

Pesto should never be cooked, so place the gnocchi in a warm bowl and dress them as you would a salad with the pesto then serve.

PROCIDA LADIES' SPAGHETTI AL PESTO DI LIMONE

❖❖❖

SPAGHETTI WITH LEMON PESTO FROM PROCIDA

PREP	30 minutes
SERVINGS	4–6 (allow 90–100g/ 3–3½ oz) of boxed spaghetti per person

3 large organic lemons, ideally from Procida
50 ml (1¾ fl oz/3½ tablespoons) lemon juice (from about 2 lemons)
10 g (½ oz) flat-leaf parsley (or basil)
5 g (⅛ oz) mint
1 garlic clove
pinch of salt
pinch of dried chilli flakes
50 ml (1¾ fl oz/3½ tablespoons) extra-virgin olive oil
50 g (1¾ oz) Italian pine nuts (or walnuts)
100 g (3½ oz) Parmigiano Reggiano (or pecorino), grated
90–100 g (3–3½ ox) spaghetti

Procida, a tiny little island just off Naples, was the location for *The Talented Mr Ripley* film and was awarded Italy's Capital for Culture for 2022. Despite the fame and attention, village life continues. Adriana, Antonietta, Enza, Maria and Teresa are neighbours and friends through the local choir who all share a love of cooking. Originally they demonstrated three recipes, which you can watch on Pasta Grannies, and this is the one that is brilliant for unexpected guests, or when you want to cook something really quick that tastes like a long weekend in Italy.

Adriana remembers in her childhood: 'My mother used to make this pesto in winter, because that is when lemons are ready to be picked. We'd forage the pine cones in the summer, then come the cold weather we'd dry the pine nuts near the fireplace before using them in this pesto. We added parsley and mint, because basil is a summer herb, but of course you can use that too. And, you know, in those days we didn't use Parmigiano – we made this pesto with pecorino cheese.'

Lemons in this part of the world are large, sweet and fragrant. These days, one can buy Amalfi lemons (which are very similar to the Procida ones) quite easily, but if you are using regular lemons, you may want to experiment with the acidity by reducing the amount of juice and adding a little more water. Meyer lemons can also be substituted.

Start by peeling the lemons; you only want the skin. A great way to remove the pith from the peel is to use a filleting knife, which has flexible blade. Anchor the peel pith side up with a finger, then with the other hand press and slither the knife horizontally under the pith (away from your fingers, please), leaving the zesty skin.

Chop the rinds finely. Strain the lemon juice to remove pips. Rough chop the parsley, mint and garlic and blitz all these together in a food processor with a pinch of salt, the chilli flakes and the oil until smooth. Roughly chop the nuts, add them to the mix and blitz again until you have a rough paste. Add half the cheese and give it a quick zhuzh. Taste for acidity and, if needed, add tablespoons of water to adjust.

Bring a large pan of salted water to the boil and cook the spaghetti for the time indicated on the packet. In the meantime take a large salad bowl and dollop in the pesto. Dilute with a ladle of hot pasta water to make it more of a sauce. Drain your pasta, keeping some of the pasta water. Toss the pasta with the pesto, adding in the rest of the cheese and adding more hot pasta water if necessary so the sauce coats the spaghetti.

Serve immediately. This should be on your regular recipe roster!

two

vegetables

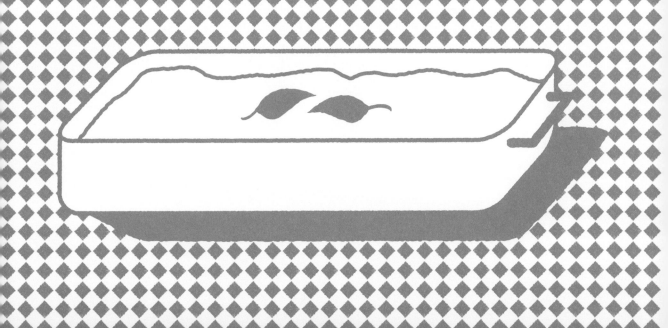

AGATA AND CLELIA'S GNOCCHI LUNGHI CON ZUCCHINI

◆◆◆

SPAGHETTI-STYLE PASTA WITH COURGETTES AND MINT FROM LAZIO

PREP	1½ hours
SERVINGS	4

FOR THE PASTA

300 g (10½ oz/2½ cups) 00 flour
110 g (3¾ oz) egg or 2 eggs
55 ml (1¾ fl oz) warm water,
   plus extra if necessary

FOR THE SAUCE

150 g (5 oz) guanciale, cubed
400 g (14 oz) courgettes
   (zucchini) (3 or 4, depending
   on the size), diced
2 tablespoons finely chopped
   mint leaves

TO SERVE

60–80 g (2–2¾ oz) Pecorino
   Romano, grated

Gnocchi lunghi look like pici or umbricelli from further north in Tuscany and Umbria. But Agata and Clelia live in Lazio, south of Rome, where the dough and the name are different. The women are sisters-in-law, who had never cooked together before I filmed them. Their granddaughter is a fan of Pasta Grannies and persuaded them to appear on the show. Agata is a *contadina* (market gardener), while Clelia has always worked as a cook in various restaurants and now helps in the family restaurant, Locanda Del Principe.

Gnocchi lunghi are an ideal shape for a novice pasta maker. It helps to have a spray water bottle to hand to lightly spritz the board while you roll out the pasta, as it will 'grip' the board better. Don't make it sodden though! Guanciale is cured pork cheek, which has plenty of fat and a great flavour. If you cannot find it, use unsmoked pancetta for this recipe.

Make the egg pasta dough as described on page 11, swapping one egg for 55 ml (1¾ fl oz) of water. Leave the dough, covered, to rest for at least 30 minutes.

Cut off a walnut-in-its-shell size piece of pasta dough. Place it on your board and roll out a string of pasta using flat palms, in the same way you would make a plasticine snake. It should be about 30 cm (12 in) long and no more than 3 mm in diameter. Lay the gnocchi lunghi out individually, not in a pile, so that they do not stick together.

To make the sauce, put the guanciale in a sauté pan over a medium-low heat (without any oil) and leave the meat to render its fat. Stir the pieces regularly to make sure they do not brown too quickly. If necessary, add a dash of water; this helps the meat to cook for longer and keep it firm and moist while releasing its fat. If you are using pancetta, remember it has less fat than guanciale and so needs a bit of help: add a tablespoon of water at the beginning to kickstart the 'I want the fat in the pan, not the meat' process.

After about 10 minutes the meat will have browned and have crispy edges. Remove the pieces from the pan and set aside. Use the lovely fat to sauté your courgettes over a medium heat for 4 minutes or so until the pieces are soft.

Recipe continued next page →   **VEGETABLES**

Recipe continued →

In the meantime, bring a large saucepan of salted water to the boil. Chuck in the gnocchi lunghi and cook them for 1–5 minutes, depending on the thickness. The thinner they are, the faster they will cook. Taste-test them every minute or so to check when they are done the way you like them. Remove about 100 ml (3½ fl oz/scant ½ cup) of pasta water, then drain everything.

Add the pasta to the sauté pan. Toss the pasta with the courgettes and 1 tablespoon of the mint and sauté the mixture for a minute or so. If you feel the pasta is drying out too much, add a bit of pasta water.

To serve, scatter over the rest of the mint and the grated Pecorino Romano.

ANNA MARIA'S CRAFUNCINS DA ULA VERDA

◆◆◆

'LEAN' SPINACH RAVIOLI FROM SOUTH TYROL

Anna Maria lives in a popular ski resort and worked in a clothes shop before she retired. She is now a shining light in the local amateur dramatics group and has the time for her main love – cooking. She keeps bags of these ravioli in her freezer for friends and neighbours to help themselves. These crafuncins are 'lean' because they are meatless, and Anna Maria omits the ricotta which is sometimes included; 'I want to be able to taste the spinach,' she says. Traditionally the dough includes rye flour, but Anna Maria prefers farro – emmer in America – as it's easier to handle.

PREP	1½–2 hours
MAKES	32 ravioli

FOR THE PASTA

125 g (4 oz/1 cup) 00 flour
125 g (4 oz/1 cup) farro flour
55 g (2 oz) egg (or 1 egg), beaten
10 g (⅓ oz) olive oil
70 ml (2⅓ fl oz/scant 5 tablespoons) tepid water
pinch of salt

FOR THE FILLING

30 g (1 oz) butter
50 g (1¾ oz) onion, finely diced
15 g (½ oz) 0 flour
25 ml (¾ fl oz) water or vegetable stock (enough to slacken the roux mixture a bit)
200 g (7 oz) frozen chopped spinach, defrosted
nutmeg, to taste
25 g (1 oz) grated Parmigiano Reggiano
salt, to taste

TO SERVE

100 g (3½ oz) butter
50 g (1¾ oz) Parmigiano, grated (traditionally, an aged goat's cheese called ziger would be used)
sage leaves, crisped in a little olive oil (optional)

First, make the pasta dough. Mix the flours together and place them on your pasta board. Make a well and place the egg, oil, water, and salt in the middle. Use a fork to scramble the liquids and then to draw in the flour. When the liquid can no longer run, break up the well and make a ball of dough. Knead it for 10 minutes until smooth. Rest the dough in a covered bowl for 30 minutes. Thanks to the oil and farro flour, this is a soft moist dough that can be a tad sticky, but don't be tempted to add extra flour to the board otherwise you'll have difficulty sealing the ravioli.

Anna Maria uses an electric roller for her pasta dough, which is good fun but it's only worth buying if you are going to make large amounts, regularly. So stick with a rolling pin and roll out the dough to a thickness of 2 mm. Use a 7.5 cm (3 in) pastry cutter to stamp out rounds; if you are careful, you should be able to achieve 32 pieces. Remove the extra pasta from around the discs; this allows you to pick them up easily.

To make the filling, melt the butter in a frying pan over a medium heat, add the onion with a pinch of salt and sauté for about 7 minutes until soft and translucent. Stir in the flour, then add the water or stock to make a thick roux. Fry for a couple of minutes then add the chopped spinach. Season the mixture with salt and plenty of grated nutmeg and cook for about 10 minutes until it is very thick. Transfer to a bowl and leave it to cool a little before adding the grated cheese. Use a stick blender to puree the mixture – it has to be smooth enough to pipe easily.

A piping bag is helpful for portion control and speedy dosing on the pasta. Take a spatula and transfer the contents to a bag. If you don't have one, don't worry, just use a couple of teaspoons to dollop a shelled-walnut quantity of spinach filling onto one side of each pasta circle.

Recipe continued next page →   **VEGETABLES**

Gently pick one up and fold one half over the other with the filling, to make a *mezzaluna* (a half-moon shape) ravioli. Make sure the edges match and squeeze them shut.

If the pasta starts getting a little dry, use a water spray bottle to lightly mist your circles before closing them. Spread the crafuncins, so they don't touch, on a tray; flip them over every 30 minutes if you are not cooking them immediately. They freeze well: place the tray flat in on the freezer shelf, and once frozen, decant them into bags and seal. They should be eaten within the month.

When you're ready to serve, melt the butter in a small non-stick pan and fry it until it is golden but not burned.

Bring a pan of salted water to the boil, add the crafuncins and simmer for a couple of minutes. Scoop them out with a spider and arrange them on a warmed platter. Sprinkle them with grated Parmigiano and pour over the browned butter. Serve immediately with crispy sage leaves crisped in a little oil, if you like.

CATERINA'S TAGLIATELLE CON MELANZANE E RICOTTA SALATA

◆◆◆

TAGLIATELLE WITH AUBERGINE AND SALTED RICOTTA FROM SICILY

PREP	1 hour
SERVINGS	4

We were standing in 91-year-old Caterina's walled vegetable garden, admiring its views and verdancy, when one of her grandsons said, 'We sometimes find pieces of Islamic pottery when we're digging through the soil, which considering the shape of this space makes us think it's been in use as a garden since those times'. Sicily was an Emirate over 900 years ago and it has been tilled and tended all that time; no wonder Caterina's veggies taste great.

Caterina also keeps a flock of chickens, so she likes to use their eggs in her pasta; it makes a firm dough. Semolina flour is more usually mixed with water, so the choice is yours.

Some of you will think, 'Oh, this is pasta alla Norma'; yes it is, except housewives like Caterina have been making the most of their veg gardens long before an enterprising restaurant came up with the name. Caterina also salts her own ricotta. She buys it fresh from the local shepherd and, once it has drained properly, she covers it in salt, wraps it in muslin and leaves it to dry further in the fridge for a few days before unwrapping it and leaving it to air-dry for several weeks.

Don't make this with insipid supermarket veg; it's worth waiting for when everything is in season and buying the produce at your local farmer's market.

FOR THE PASTA

250 g (9 oz/scant 1⅔ cups) semolina flour
110 g (3¾ oz) eggs (or 2 medium eggs)
15 g (½ oz) water (or omit the eggs and use 125 g/4 oz water)

FOR THE SAUCE

1 onion, thinly sliced
1 garlic clove, thinly sliced
4 large, ripe and flavoursome tomatoes, chopped
2 medium aubergines (eggplants), halved lengthways
plenty of neutral vegetable oil, for frying
3 tablespoons extra-virgin olive oil
25 g (1 oz) basil leaves
salt

TO SERVE

100 g (3½ oz) ricotta salata, sharp feta or pecorino

Combine the flour and eggs in a large bowl or on your wooden board, leaving the water to one side until – or if – it is needed.

When you have a formed a ball of dough, knead it for 10 minutes until smooth and bouncy. Leave it to relax in a covered container for at least 30 minutes.

While the pasta dough is resting, make the sauce. Heat a sauté pan over a medium heat, add the onion, garlic and chopped tomatoes, season with a little salt and leave the sauce to cook down gently for 15 minutes. Don't add the oil at this stage.

Slice your aubergine halves into 1 cm (¾ in)-thick half rounds. Heat plenty of neutral oil in a small frying pan (enough to cover a slice of aubergine). When you stick a wooden skewer into the oil it should sizzle. Fry the aubergine slices 2 or 3 at a time (don't overcrowd the pan) for about 2 minutes until they are golden and place them on paper towels to drain.

Puree the cooked tomatoes – ideally through a food mill so you remove the skins – then put the sauce back in the pan along with the olive oil, basil leaves and half of the cooked aubergine slices.

When you are ready, roll out your pasta dough to a thickness of 1–2 mm and leave it to rest for 10 minutes. Sprinkle then smooth some flour over its surface, so it won't stick when you fold it over to form a loose log. Take a sharp chef's knife and cut 7 mm-wide ribbons. Shake the tagliatelle out and leave them to dry a little on the board, 5 minutes is fine.

Cook the tagliatelle in plenty of salted boiling water for 5–7 minutes until al dente – taste test for doneness, then drain thoroughly. Spoon some of the tomato sauce over a platter, then transfer half of the tagliatelle to the platter. Add more sauce on top with some more basil leaves. Add the remaining tagliatelle and sauce and toss everything together. Arrange the rest of the fried aubergines on top.

To serve, grate plenty of ricotta salata over everything and let everyone tuck in.

ELISABETTA'S FILEJA CON CIPOLLE DI TROPEA

◆◆◆

MACCHERONI PASTA WITH TROPEA ONIONS FROM CALABRIA

PREP	45 minutes, plus resting time
SERVINGS	4
DRIED PASTA ALTERNATIVE	Spaghetti

FOR THE PASTA

250 g (9 oz/scant 1⅔ cups) 00
    or plain (all-purpose) flour, plus
    extra for dusting
50 g (1¾ oz/⅓ cup)
    semolina flour
about 150 ml (5 fl oz/⅔ cup)
    warm water

FOR THE DRESSING

2 tablespoons extra-virgin olive oil
6–8 red onions, peeled and thinly
    sliced (you want a total of
    700 g/1 lb 9 oz prepped onion)
1 teaspoon salt
dried peperoncino flakes (to taste)
200 g (7 oz) passata
1 heaped teaspoon sun-dried
    pepper paste or biber salçasi

TO SERVE

grated pecorino, to taste
a handful of basil leaves

The women of Tropea in Calabria have a reputation for being independently minded and good at business; Elisabetta is a charming example. She was one of five siblings who ended up taking over their brother's restaurant in Tropea 'for fun, because he was away at sea for long periods'. She was in charge of the kitchen for 60 years and this was one of her popular pasta dishes using the beautiful sweet red onions for which Tropea is famous. Elisabetta says they're sweet because they grow so close to the sea; certainly the sandy soils and moderate climate help. Even those who usually swerve the raw onions in a salad find these palatable.

If you want to make your own sun-dried pepper paste, start by growing the round tomato-shaped Topepo variety. Boil the peppers until tender, peel off the skin, put the flesh through a food mill to remove the seeds, stir in some salt (taste it, don't go mad) and spread out the mixture to dry in really hot sun on a wide tray with edges so you can clip over some fine netting to keep out the bugs. It will reduce in volume considerably as the juices evaporate over several days. Alternatively, buy some Turkish biber salçasi which is an acceptable substitute for the Topepo paste; one cannot find the Topepo paste even in other parts of Italy.

Make the pasta dough as described on page 13.

To form the fileja, you will need a square-sided metal rod called a ferro; failing that, a wooden kebab skewer will do nicely – it should be about 30 cm (12 in) long.

Cut off a small amount of pasta dough and roll it out into a rope about the thickness of a pencil. Snip into 12 cm (4¾ in) lengths. Elisabetta likes to wrap each one around her rod (hers happens to be bamboo) and roll it gently with flat palms, which start together in the middle of the rod and move outwards. Remember to keep everything well floured to stop the pasta from sticking to the skewer.

Don't press too hard and do not elongate the pasta too much making it very thin on the rod or skewer, as this will also result in the dough sticking.

Once you have an imperfect 'tube' of pasta, gently place it in one hand and twist and twizzle the ferro or skewer back and forth, gently easing it from the pasta. Don't hold the pasta hard. You will be left with tubes that look a bit like leaky or incomplete bucatini (long pasta with a hole through the length).

Put the olive oil, sliced onions, salt and peperoncino flakes in a medium sauté pan, stir well and start cooking the mixture over a low heat. After 15 minutes, add the passata and pepper paste. Keep cooking and add a splash of water as needed to prevent the onions from sticking or burning.

Recipe continued next page →

VEGETABLES

The sauce is ready when the onions are pale, mushy and reduced to almost a paste. This will take a good 40 minutes.

Cook the pasta in plenty of salted boiling water for about 5 minutes, and in the meantime reheat the sauce in a sauté pan (add a little water if it looks dry). Once the pasta is al dente, transfer it with the spider sieve from the boiling water into the sauté pan and finish cooking. Add a little pasta cooking water if necessary. Take the pan off the heat and stir through the grated pecorino and freshly shredded basil. Serve on warmed plates with more peperoncino if you like things spicy.

IRMA'S STRINGOZZI CON SUGO DI POMODORI

◆◆◆

STRINGOZZI WITH TOMATO, CAPER AND OLIVE SAUCE FROM LAZIO

PREP	1 hour, plus resting time
SERVINGS	5–6

FOR THE PASTA

150 g (5 oz/1¼ cups) semolina flour
350 g (12 oz/2¾ cups) 00 flour
2 g (½ teaspoon) fine salt
55 g (2 oz) egg or 1 egg
20 g (¾ oz) olive oil
175 ml (5 fl oz/⅔ cup) warm water

FOR THE SAUCE

500 g (1 lb 2 oz) cherry tomatoes
10 large black olives
1 garlic clove, halved
5 basil leaves
plenty of extra-virgin olive oil
15 salt-packed capers, rinsed
1 tinned anchovy fillet, drained
    of oil, finely chopped
salt, to taste (you may not need it)

TO SERVE

50 g (1¾ oz) Pecorino Romano,
    grated

This long continuous pasta loop has several names: *sthridhlja* in Calabria, *pasta alla mugnaia* in Abruzzo, *dores* in Basilicata. Culinary historians say Albanian refugees brought the pasta shape to Italy with them in the 15th century. In Casperia, where Irma lives, these loops are called *stringozzi* and there are no connections to the southern *Arbëreshë* communities. Meanwhile, in Umbria, *stringozzi* are thin tagliolini ribbons so named because they resemble shoelaces. It's a good example of the head-spinning complexity of pasta shapes and names in Italy.

And Irma has made her own contribution: decades ago, long before the internet had been invented and local knowledge became global, Irma picked up her dough and experimented with how to stretch her stringozzi quicker. It turns out her technique is amazingly similar to pulled Chinese wheat noodles, but she had no idea.

To make the pasta, sift the two flours and the salt together on the board and make a well. Scramble the egg, oil and water together in a jug or bowl then pour into the centre of the well. Use a fork to draw the flour wall gradually into the liquid, before finally mixing the ingredients together to obtain a ball of dough. Knead for 10–15 minutes until smooth and very bouncy. Divide the dough in two equal pieces and make perfect balls of each. Flatten them into thick discs and poke a hole in the middle of each so they look like doughnuts. Oil the dough and put them in a plastic bag with no air to rest for a good 2 hours.

To make the pasta, first watch Irma's video. Then, twirl a disc around your finger to make the hole in the middle larger. When you can get all five fingers through the hole, gently grasp the dough with one hand and start to stretch it with the other so it looks like a bicycle tyre. Keeping it well oiled, keep stretching the dough until it's about a 25 cm (9¾ in) hoop. Take it between both hands and smack it gently on the board while very gently pulling the dough to extend it. Turn it after every couple of slaps. Eventually it will be large enough to make a double loop. Keep going, slapping and turning, making sure the dough and your hands stay well oiled. It shouldn't break, but if it does, just squeeze and pinch the dough back together.

Most other cooks making this shape keep the dough loop on the board and roll the rope thinner with flat palms, working their way around the loop several times. And you can do this too if it's easier. Remember to always go in the same direction so the dough loop gets evenly thinner.

Recipe continued next page →

Recipe continued →

Once the slapped loopy-loop is 2–3 cm (¾–1¼ in) in diameter, unloop it and roll your way around it as described above, until it is about the thickness of a pencil. Keep your hands well oiled. Keep the rest of the dough you are not working on spread out.

Then comes the final step of making the dough-loop thinner. Cup some semolina in one hand and with the other, loop the pasta as a double strand over the semolina hand until there isn't any loop left. Now gently squeeze and pull the strands through your hands, turning the loops in a circle to continue the thinning process. Use semolina to stop the pasta from sticking. When the stringozzi strand is about 5 mm (¼ in) thick, it's ready. Repeat with the other disc.

Phew! The dressing is easy. Halve your cherry tomatoes, and pit and halve the olives (don't be tempted to buy them ready-pitted – they are never as good quality). Add the toms to a sauté pan with the halved garlic and basil. Pour over enough olive oil to cover the basil leaves so they don't go black while cooking. Place the pan over a medium heat and gently fry the mixture, stirring it regularly, for about 5 minutes. When the tomatoes have released their watery juices and there is a bit of sauce forming, add the olives followed by the capers and anchovy.

Let everything simmer for about 10 minutes. Check the seasoning and see if the sauce needs more salt. If the sauce starts getting too thick, add a splash of water.

While your sauce is simmering, bring a large saucepan of salted water to the boil and cook the stringozzi for about 3 minutes once the water has returned to the boil. The pasta floating to the top doesn't mean the strands are cooked (unless you like them very al dente). Lift them up; they should hang limply but not be sticky.

Nibble one (okay, that means breaking the loop but you're going to have to do that to eat it anyway). Use a spider to scoop the pasta from the water, place the loops in the tomato sauce and continue to cook everything over a low heat for another 2 minutes. Finish the dish with grated pecorino and serve warm.

LUCIA AND PINO'S BUCATINI ALLA TRAPANESE

◆◆◆

BUCATINI WITH RAW TOMATO SAUCE FROM SICILY

PREP	1–1½ hours
SERVINGS	4

DRIED PASTA ALTERNATIVE	360 g (12½ oz) bucatini

The flour mill Mulino Fiaccati di Roccapalumba feels hidden and secret, perched on the side of a tumbling river bed, deep down in a boulder-strewn ravine and surrounded by prickly pears in the fields above. It's hard to imagine that once, in the days before machinery, the wheat fields were full of farmworkers who would come to eat their lunch at the mill. This is the region of Sicily where the commercial production of dried pasta was first noted in the 12th century.

These days, Pino is the custodian of the mill and he showed us a wonderful wooden contraption used to extrude pasta dough through a bronze die to form bucatini (spaghetti with a hole through the middle). If you are a pasta fan you can do the same by buying a hand-operated torchio or an attachment for your food mixer. The pasta needs durum wheat flour, the slightly gritty kind called semola in Italian, and water. To stop it from sticking as it goes through the extruder, the dough needs to be a little drier than when you roll it out by hand. You should allow 40 g (1½ oz) of water (or 40 ml/1¼ fl oz/2½ tablespoons, but weighing it is more accurate) for every 100 g (3½ oz/⅔ cup) of flour. In other words, 40% hydration. This will make a stiff dough. Or, buy a packet of bucatini; look for good quality pasta to make the most of this very simple recipe.

Pino and Lucia's recipe is a Sicilian summer in a bowl. Sunshine is one of the ingredients you will need for this dish; the kind that shimmers as the cicadas' strumming makes your eardrums feel they are being electrocuted. Pick basil that has also been sun-blasted, as this brings out the clove fragrance of the herb. And, of course, choose good-quality tomatoes; look out for fleshy Italian varieties like Roma, San Marzano and Pachino.

Recipe continued next page → **VEGETABLES**

FOR THE PASTA

400 g (14 oz/3 ⅓ cups) semola
  durum wheat flour
160 g (5½ fl oz/⅔ cup) warm
  water
1 g (¼ teaspoon) fine salt

FOR THE SAUCE

1 kg (2 lb 4 oz) whole, very
  ripe tomatoes; after prep this
  becomes about 500 g (1 lb 2 oz)
1–2 fresh large garlic cloves
1 teaspoon fine salt
6 tablespoons extra-virgin olive oil
20 basil leaves, hand shredded
80–120 g (2¾–4¼ oz)
  pecorino, grated

Recipe continued →

To make the pasta dough, combine the flour, water and salt in a bowl. Once you have a ball of dough, knead it for 5–8 minutes on a board until it is smooth and bouncy and no longer breaks apart. This is a good workout! Resting the dough isn't necessary. Run it through your extrusion machine using your bucatini die, cutting off 20 cm (8 in) lengths. Place them on a mesh rack or floured baking sheet and spread out in a single layer, until you are ready to cook them.

Now for the sauce. Cut a cross in the tip of every tomato (i.e. the opposite end from the stem, which should be removed if present) with a sharp knife. Bring a saucepan full of water to the boil and blanch the tomatoes for 30 seconds. Transfer the fruit to a bowl filled with cold water to stop the cooking. Over a bowl, peel off the skin from each tomato, halve and scoop out the seeds. Keep the flesh and the juice.

Cut the tomatoes into 1 cm (½ in) cubes and place them in a heatproof pan with the juice. Turn the garlic into mush by chopping it finely with the salt. Stir it into the tomatoes with the olive oil and shredded basil leaves.

Place the pan of mixed ingredients in direct hot sun for 30 minutes. And if your sun isn't hot enough? Warm (don't bake) the toms in a preheated oven at 50°C/122°F for 20–30 minutes. This will help develop the flavours.

While the tomato mixture is warming up, bring a large pan of salted water to the boil. Time the pasta cooking so that it is ready when the sauce is. This means following the instructions on the pasta packet, or allowing 5 minutes of cooking time for the fresh pasta before nibbling a strand every couple of minutes until you are satisfied the strands are al dente.

Drain the bucatini very well and combine with your sauce and the pecorino. Serve immediately.

VEGETABLES

MARIA'S BUCATINI CON I TENERUMI

◆◆◆

BUCATINI PASTA SOUP WITH SUMMER SQUASH FROM PALERMO

PREP 1 hour
SERVINGS 4–5

We met Maria through her seniors' social club in the suburbs of Palermo, Sicily. 'I'm single; I worked so hard for my independence I didn't want to give it up. And this club is great source of friendship.' One of her pals has a secret garden, right on the beach. Step through a door and down a corridor and there's a courtyard stuffed full of flowers and vegetables. The shade is provided by a summer squash called cucuzza in Palermo (and 'Sicilian snakes' in the UK). These grow at an incredible rate, and don't mind if you snip off their young leaves and tendrils, which are called tenerumi locally. The fruit can grow up to 2 metres (6 feet) in length. An obvious swap is normal courgettes (zucchini) which also have edible leaves. Truth be told, they don't have a distinct flavour and I suspect this dish is a consequence of keeping a rampant plant under control – and is a good hot summer alternative to cool-weather-loving spinach.

FOR THE TOMATO SAUCE

500 g (1 lb 2 oz) flavoursome ripe tomatoes, rinsed
glug of extra-virgin olive oil, plus extra to serve
3 garlic cloves, halved
15 g (½ oz) basil leaves
salt, to taste

FOR THE SOUP

300 g (10½ oz) tenerumi, chard or romaine lettuce
250 g (9 oz) cucuzza squash or courgette (zucchini), cut into bite-sized chunks
1 litre (34 fl oz/4¼ cups) water
1 teaspoon salt
300 g (10½ oz) boxed spaghetti, or bucatini no.5
50 g (1¾ oz) caciocavallo cheese, cut into small cubes

Quarter the tomatoes for the sauce, then run the pieces through a food mill to obtain a lovely smooth sauce with no skins or seeds. Give the seedy pulp to your chickens if you have them – they love it.

Heat up plenty of olive oil in a saucepan over a medium heat, add the halved garlic and let it infuse the oil for 5 minutes. Remove the pieces if you don't like whole garlic in your soup, otherwise just add the tomatoes before the garlic becomes golden. Season with salt, chuck in your basil, cover and simmer for 20 minutes.

In the meantime, trim your greens of any tough ends and, in the case of tenerumi, peel the stems of prickles and tough skins, and remove the tendrils. Chop them up roughly.

Pour the 1 litre (34 fl oz/4¼ cups) of water into another pan, add half a teaspoon of salt, bring to the boil and cook the squash cubes and greens for about 5 minutes until everything is tender. Don't drain it!

Snap or chop the bucatini or spaghetti into matchstick lengths.

Once the tomato sauce tastes fragrant with basil, pour it into the pan of greens. Add the pasta and cook everything for roughly the time indicated on the pasta box (pasta cooked in sauce sometimes takes longer). When the pasta is done to your liking, turn off the heat and let it cool for 5 minutes before adding the cheese.

Dribble a generous amount of spicy extra-virgin olive oil over each serving.

MARIETTA'S TAGLIATELLE CON SUGO ALLA CONTADINA

◆◆◆

TAGLIATELLE WITH FARMER'S SAUCE FROM CALABRIA

PREP	1 hour
SERVINGS	4–6
DRIED PASTA ALTERNATIVE	Tagliatelle

'Is this a meal you would eat on Sundays?' We were filming 99-year-old Marietta make pork meatballs with tagliatelle, and it was the first time we'd met her. 'Ah, signora!' Marietta replied, 'you cannot kill a pig that often! We would eat this once, maybe twice a year!'

The yearly pig belonged to Marietta's uncle with whom she lived, along with her mother and siblings. When she was three years old, her dad left Calabria for Argentina and never came back. Everyone had to work on the farm to survive and three-year-old Marietta's task was to take care of the sheep: 'I thought it was fun, I was joining in with the grown-ups.'

As she grew older, her list of responsibilities grew: she milked the sheep, took water on her head to thirsty farmworkers and tended the *orto* (vegetable garden). She still loves gardening – she has lots of pots on her daughter's roof terrace in Rome where she lives most of the year. She met her husband Peppino at the procession of Saint Gaetano, a yearly event where all the villages in the area got together. 'It was the main way to meet boys!' Marietta grinned.

'And then I became a chair maker.' Serrastretta is surrounded by beech and chestnut forests and it is the centre of handmade wood chairs. 'I made two early in the morning, then I went to the fields. It took me one and a half hours walking to get there. I'd take sheep manure compost with me, then bring back onions, tomatoes, beans, whatever was growing. Then I had to make two more chairs.'

'But we had to make everything. This cloth is made with *ginestra* – broom. We took the twigs down to the river to soak for days, then we laid them in the sun. Then we turned it into a textile.' This beautiful soft cloth had several uses. 'Fold it like this and it helps keep bowls and things on my head. I use it as an apron, I tuck it like this, and of course it's for drying my vegetables.'

So, this recipe is a not really a recipe at all; it's an echo of Marietta's *orto*, her countryside and the seasons. Courgette (zucchini), borlotti (cranberry) beans and field mushrooms can all be added (though not all at once). If you cannot find a vegetable in the list below, don't fuss; do as Marietta does and find something fresh and at its best. And yes, very occasionally, you might want to include some precious pancetta.

Recipe next page →

VEGETABLES

FOR THE PASTA

400 g (14 oz/3⅓ cups) semolina
  flour
190–200 ml (7 fl oz/ scant 1 cup)
  warm water
pinch of salt

FOR THE SAUCE

extra-virgin olive oil, for frying
1 small onion, finely diced
1 carrot, finely diced
1 celery stalk, finely diced
1 garlic clove, finely chopped
small pinch of dried red chilli flakes
2 tablespoons water
500 g (1 lb 2 oz) greens, such as
  chard, borage, cardella, chicory,
  dandelion and *cime di rapa*
  or broccoli
250 g (9 oz) tomatoes (passata
  or fresh chopped tomatoes when
  in season)
a handful of mixed herbs, such as
  wild fennel, parsley, sage, basil,
  marjoram or oregano

TO SERVE

extra-virgin olive oil
grated pecorino (optional)

Make the pasta dough as described on page 13. Having let it rest for at least 30 minutes, roll it out to a thickness of 2 mm. Dust and smooth some flour over the surface, then roll a loose, long log about 7 cm (2¾ in) wide. Use a sharp, straight-bladed knife to cut the log into 5 mm (¼ in)-wide tagliatelle ribbons.

To make the sauce, add a slug of olive oil to a large sauté or frying pan and place it over a medium heat. Add the onion, carrot and celery and fry gently for 7–10 minutes until soft. Add the garlic and dried red chilli flakes and a pinch of salt and cook for another minute or so, making sure the garlic doesn't brown.

Pour in the water, then add the greens. Give them a good stir and add the tomatoes. Chop up the herbs so you have a good 2 tablespoons and stir this mixture into the sauce. Continue to simmer for 20 minutes or so.

Bring a saucepan of salted water to the boil and cook the tagliatelle for a minute or two; you want it to be al dente. Use a spider to scoop it out and dump it into the sauce. Sauté everything for another minute, and ladle in a bit of pasta water into the pan if the mixture looks a bit dry.

Serve immediately. Finish with a drizzle of olive oil and grated pecorino if you fancy it.

SPERANDINA'S LASAGNA CON ASPARAGI

♦♦♦

ASPARAGUS LASAGNA FROM LE MARCHE

PREP	2 hours
SERVINGS	6–8

FOR THE PASTA

300 g (10½ oz/2½ cups) 00 flour
165 g (5¾ oz) egg or 3 eggs

FOR THE BÉCHAMEL SAUCE

40 g (1½ oz) unsalted butter
40 g (1½ oz) 0 flour
750 ml (25 fl oz/3 cups) full-fat milk
nutmeg
salt

FOR THE FILLING

900 g (2 lb) trimmed fresh
   or frozen asparagus, sliced
   in widthways
800 ml (27 fl oz/3½ cups)
   béchamel sauce (above)
300 g (10½ oz) cow's milk
   mozzarella (the block style
   is fine) cut into small cubes
100 g (3½ oz) grated Parmigiano
   Reggiano

Sperandina's children and grandchildren work locally, so they all come for lunch every day; and of course she is more than happy to cook for them. This lasagna is one she serves in spring when there is plenty of wild asparagus on her hillside.

Sperandina lives at the foot of Monti Sibilini in Le Marche. Its most famous lasagna is vincisgrassi, which now has an official recipe; the meat ragù is enriched with chicken offal. But Sperandina refers to this dish as vincisgrassi because locally that is what all lasagna are called. This is the joy of pasta names! Call it what you want and do try it. You can use frozen asparagus instead of fresh, but bear in mind it's more watery. If you would like the dish to be more green rather than khaki, add a few spinach leaves to the vegetables before pureeing them.

Make the pasta dough as described on page 11 and leave it, covered, for a good 30 minutes. Roll it out to a thickness of 1–2 mm and cut it to fit a 32 x 25 x 8 cm (12½ 9¾ x 3 in) baking dish or roasting tin. You should be able to create 4 layers with this amount of dough.

Make the béchamel sauce. Melt the butter in a non-stick saucepan over a medium heat. Add the flour and use a wooden spoon to beat the two ingredients together and form a roux. Cook it for a couple of minutes then gradually pour in the milk, stirring all the while. Season with salt and plenty of freshly grated nutmeg.

Bring some salted water to the boil in a saucepan. Chuck in the asparagus bottom halves and simmer for 3 minutes then add the top halves, which don't take as long to cook. Once tender (there should be no resistance when you stab a piece with a sharp pointed knife), drain and reserve the water. Blitz the asparagus with a stick blender, adding as much of the asparagus water as you need to form an easily spreadable puree. If using frozen asparagus, plunge them in boiling salted water and wait for the water to come back to a full rolling boil, then check frequently for doneness. They tend to be more watery so it will be easier to make a smooth puree without too much additional cooking water. Taste the puree and adjust its seasoning; not enough salt will make the lasagna taste a tad flat.

Have ready a large bowl of very cold salted water. Blanch the pasta rectangles one by one in a large pot of boiling salted water for 1 minute, then remove them with a spider strainer and plunge them into the water. Once cooled, place them on a perfume-free tea towel to remove the excess water.

Now assemble the dish. Start with a layer of béchamel, then pasta, a thin layer of béchamel, then puree of asparagus, a sprinkle of Parmigiano and mozzarella, then repeat until you have 4 layers of pasta. Aim to finish off all the asparagus at this stage.

Finish the top with a smoothing of béchamel, and plenty of Parmigiano and mozzarella.

Bake in the oven for about 45 minutes and, if the top is not browned and crusty, turn on the top grill and let it heat up before placing the lasagna under it. Leave it there for as long as it takes for the cheese to colour.

Remove from the oven and let the lasagna cool for around 15 minutes before serving.

TERESA'S MACCHERONI CON OLIVE VERDE

◆◆◆

MACCHERONI WITH GREEN OLIVES FROM CALABRIA

PREP	1 hour–1 hour 20 minutes
SERVINGS	4
DRIED PASTA ALTERNATIVE	Bucatini

FOR THE PASTA

300 g (10½ oz/2½ cups) semolina flour
135–145 ml (4½–5 fl oz/generous ½ cup–⅔ cup) warm water

FOR THE SAUCE

350 g (12 oz) green olives (stone in)
500 g (1 lb 2 oz) ripe, flavoursome tomatoes
4 tablespoons extra-virgin olive oil
1 onion, diced
1 fresh red chilli, finely to taste
1 bunch of basil leaves

TO SERVE (OPTIONAL)

grated pecorino

The village of Bivongo in Calabria has the highest number of over 90-year-olds in Italy and Teresa isn't one of them! She is a youngster of 80, a human skylark who bursts into song whenever the mood takes her, which is often.

For this recipe you need good-quality green olives. Teresa makes her own. I asked her how. 'Oh it's easy. Make sure they don't have fly damage. Wash them, cut the flesh. Use 200 g (7 oz) of salt for every 5 litres of water. The more salt, the longer the olives will last. Then I cover them with this solution and flavourings like chilli pepper, garlic and fennel flowers.' Of course, she grows and gathers everything herself.

This includes the grass stalks she uses for rolling her pasta, the Latin name of which is Ampelodesmos mauritanicus. She harvests big handfuls in the summer, which then keep her going for the year. These allow her to make long maccheroni, not that she is interested in giving her pasta a name; she calls it *pasta di casa* (homemade pasta). If you are in a hurry, use good-quality packet spaghetti or bucatini instead. Allow 90–100 g (3– 3½ oz) of pasta per person.

To make the pasta, put the flour in a bowl, make a well in it and pour in the water. Use your hands to scrunch it into a dough. Transfer it to a wooden board and knead for about 5 minutes until smooth and bouncy. There is no need to work it more. Teresa creates a rope from the main ball of dough, but you may find it easier to cut chunks off and then roll each one into a snake about 1 cm (½ in) in diameter. There is no need to be exact, but try to aim for something that looks like a smooth grissini stick.

Snip 10 cm (4 in) lengths off the rope and wrap around a bamboo skewer which should be at least 30 cm (12 in) long. If it isn't, then snip shorter lengths of dough. Your maccheroni will be shorter, but it will taste the same.

So, having made a coil around the stick, place it on the board and, using gentle downward pressure, roll the dough (and skewer) under your flat palms, starting from the middle and moving outwards. You are aiming for a long tube and you should be able to achieve this in 3 or so strokes. Do not press too hard or make the pasta too thin on the stick otherwise the dough will stick to the skewer.

Take the pasta off the skewer by holding it gently it across the palm of one hand and gently wiggling and pulling the skewer back and forth to release it from the inside of the tube. When you feel it is free, pull it out and place the pasta on the board to dry out a little while you roll the others.

Now make the sauce. Remove the stones from the olives. You can peel the flesh off the pip with a paring knife or use a cherry pipper. Make a fresh tomato sauce by putting your tomatoes through a food mill, placed over a bowl, to remove the pips and skins.

Teresa likes to use a terracotta pot for this sauce, but if you don't have one, select a heavy-bottomed sauté pan and place it over a medium heat. Add the 4 tablespoons of olive oil followed by the diced onion and soften for 7 minutes, then add the pitted green olives, chopped chilli and torn basil leaves. Fry for a few more minutes then pour in the tomato

sauce. Taste for salt – the olives will be salty, so it may not need any more. Let the sauce simmer for 20 minutes until slightly reduced.

Bring a saucepan of salted water to the boil. Add the maccheroni and give everything a good swirl. Cook for 3 minutes, then taste-test the pasta every minute or so to assess when it is done to your liking.

Strain the pasta and dump it in the sauté pan with the sauce. Cook the mixture for a minute or so more, so the pasta and sauce get to know one another.

Distribute it between 4 warmed pasta bowls and serve with grated pecorino if you wish.

three

rice & pulses

ANGELINA'S LAGANE CON CECI

◆◆◆

TAGLIATELLE PASTA WITH CHICKPEAS FROM CILENTO

PREP	1 hour, plus overnight soaking
SERVINGS	4
DRIED PASTA ALTERNATIVE	Tagliatelle

Ninety-one-year-old great, great grandmother Angelina's family home was built about the same time as the huge olive trees which surround it were planted, in the early 15th century. It is located inside the Cilento national park in Campania. The building remains unmodernised, with wide floorboards, walls darkened by smoke, and no electricity. The ground floor is for the animals; these days there is only one pig in the sty by the outside staircase leading to the living area. Her 72-year-old son (a great grandfather) shrugged as he showed us round. 'These days people don't want to eat the whole pig and they don't like the labour involved in preparing it. I don't know if we'll bother next year.'

Angelina sat by the open hearth, with a woolly hat firmly pulled over her ears; the autumn sunshine had not penetrated the thick stone walls. 'Thirteen people slept in this room; there were nine of us children,' Angelina said, 'and we had nothing to eat but a lot of happiness!'. She left school when she was 10 years old. One of her jobs was collecting chestnuts from the forests that surround the village, which were an important source of carbohydrate in poor communities.

I asked her about chickpeas (garbanzo beans) and what they meant to her. 'Ah,' she replied, 'In those days, the most important task for a wife was to have children.' A lot of children was a sign of being rich. 'So my friends and I would make a pilgrimage to the shrine of San Gerardo Majella and pray for a healthy pregnancy (he is the patron saint of mothers) and on the way back, we'd buy chickpeas.'

For this recipe, Angelina uses chickpeas from Cicerale, a nearby village which has the legume in its coat of arms. Chickpeas have been grown here since the Middle Ages and have an especially good flavour thanks to the soil and lack of irrigation. Start soaking them the day before you plan on making and serving the pasta.

FOR THE PASTA

300 g (10½ oz/2½ cups) semolina flour
55 g (2 oz) egg or 1 egg
100 ml (3½ fl oz/scant ½ cup) warm water (or less if your egg is large)

To make the chickpea (garbanzo bean) sauce, drain the soaked chickpeas and rinse them in a sieve under cold running water. Place them in a pot with the parsley sprigs, 4 tablespoons of the olive oil and enough water to cover the beans by 4 cm (1½ in). Bring to a simmer. Once the chickpeas start to soften, season them with a teaspoon of salt. Keep cooking until the chickpeas are very tender. The cooking time can take up to 1 hour or more and depends on the age and quality of the chickpeas. Remember to add more water to ensure the beans remain covered.

Recipe continued next page →   **RICE & PULSES**

FOR THE CHICKPEA SAUCE

200 g (7 oz) good-quality dried
  chickpeas (garbanzo beans),
  soaked overnight in plenty of
  cold water with 1 teaspoon salt
2 sprigs of flat-leaf parsley
  (or 1 small sprig of rosemary)
8 tablespoons extra-virgin olive oil
1 plump garlic clove, chopped
salt

TO SERVE

1 fresh red chilli (deseeded if you
  want), or dried chilli flakes

Make the pasta as described on page 11, then leave it to rest, covered, for at least 30 minutes: the longer it rests, the softer it is. If you are trying to reduce your plastic use, place the pasta in a bowl in which it is a snug fit and cover with a close-fitting lid or dampened cloth that has not been cleaned in perfumed detergent. You don't want it drying out.

When you are ready, roll out the pasta dough to a thickness of 2 mm (1/16 in), flour the sfoglia generously and fold it over into a loose log, like a carpet. Cut into 3–5 mm (1/8–1/4 in)-wide *lagane* strips (fine ribbons). It's fine to leave them on a tray while the chickpeas continue to cook, if necessary.

Meanwhile, gently fry the garlic in 2 tablespoons of the oil in a small frying pan. When you can smell the garlic and before it browns, pour it all into the chickpeas.

Add the pasta ribbons to the chickpeas, making sure there is enough liquid to accommodate all your ingredients. Continue to cook everything for about 5 minutes; how long the pasta takes to cook will depend on how thick and dry it is, so nibble one to test it after 4 minutes.

Fry a large fresh red chilli or a generous pinch of dried chilli flakes for about 3 minutes in the remaining 2 tablespoons of olive oil and pour this mixture into the chickpeas just before serving.

ANNA'S POMODORI RIPIENI DI RISO ALLA ROMANA

◆◆◆

ROMAN STUFFED TOMATOES

PREP 1–2 hours
SERVINGS 4

4 large ripe tomatoes
200 g (7 oz) risotto rice such
    as Arborio
16 basil leaves
olive oil, for seasoning and
    drizzling
4 small garlic cloves
salt and pepper

Baked rice-filled tomatoes are a classic summer dish in Rome, prepared in the cooler hours and then eaten, at room temperature, later in the day. These toms are usually baked with potato wedges, but Anna likes to add peppers to the mix too, so cooks them in a separate pan.

In Rome's greengrocers you'll find tomatoes labelled as suitable for this dish. It isn't simply a question of 'ripeness', they have also got to be flavoursome. If you are in any doubt whether your toms are flavoursome enough, you should hesitate to do this dish; but if you still want to try it, stir in a couple of tablespoons of grated pecorino or Parmigiano just before you divide the rice mixture between the tomatoes.

Preheat the oven to 175°C (325°F/gas 3).

Cut the tops off the tomatoes (keep the tops as they will be the lid) and scoop out the flesh. A food mill is a useful gadget here: plop the pulp onto the plate and crush the contents into a bowl. This removes the pips and hard bits that can form near the stalk. Or run the tomatoes through a fine sieve with a wooden spoon (less fun than using a mill). Shred the basil leaves finely and stir these into the juice with a scant teaspoon of salt, 2 tablespoons of olive oil and a couple of grinds of black pepper. Taste it; the rice is going to absorb and knock back the flavour, so you want it to be properly seasoned.

Anna's method is to soak the rice in this mixture for at least 1 hour before spooning it into the tomato shells, but I have found my rice doesn't cook very evenly when I do this, so I cheat and simmer the tomato-rice mix in a pan for 6 minutes and let it cool a little before I distribute it evenly among the 4 tomato shells, making sure not to overfill any of them.

Tuck a small garlic clove into each tomato and top with the lid. Place them in a baking dish and drizzle everything with olive oil.

Bake in the oven for 50–60 minutes.

Remove from the oven and once they are cool, remove the garlic cloves. Served warm or at room temperature; they taste even better if you can let them sit overnight.

BETTINA'S STRANGUGGI

❖❖❖

CORTALE BEAN AND PASTA SOUP FROM CALABRIA

PREP	2 hours, plus overnight soaking
SERVINGS	4–6
DRIED PASTA ALTERNATIVE	Fusilli or penne rigate

FOR THE PASTA
200 g (7 oz/1⅔ cups) semolina flour
100 g (3½ oz/⅔ cup) 0 flour
135–150 ml (4½–5 fl oz/generous ½–⅔ cup) warm water
salt

FOR THE SOUP
300 g (10½ oz) dried white cannellini beans, soaked overnight in plenty of cold water with 1 teaspoon salt
olive oil
1 large onion, chopped
2 celery sticks, including the leaves, chopped
1 kg (2 lb 4 oz) trimmed leafy greens such as chicory, Swiss chard or cabbage (any sturdy green will do)
400 g (14 oz) passata

TO SERVE
peperoncino flakes
extra-virgin olive oil

'When I was young, I was cute,' Bettina twinkled as she shared a tiny, hazy photo of herself. 'Boys would stand beneath my balcony in the evenings and serenade me. If I didn't like them, I'd pretend not to hear. Of course, if they were handsome, now that was a different story!' Bettina married her singing beau, Carlo, at the age of 20. They first met at a party celebrating the *vendemmia* (grape harvest).

Bettina comes from a family of tenant farmers, with five brothers and sisters. She had her list of jobs to do from a young age, such as fetching water and wood for the oven. She made bread for the family every week, while on the farm she helped with the olive and grape harvests. When her husband went to Switzerland to work, Bettina stayed at home raising her family and continuing with olive picking for the next 30 years.

She lives in Cortale, Calabria, where the cannellina bianca bean has a Slow Food Presidium to promote it. Bettina likes to use this variety because the bean cooks well; it is thin skinned and has a slightly floury texture. Ordinary white cannellini beans are a good swap.

Cook the soaked beans: drain and add them to a large pan of lightly salted boiling water until tender but not mushy. How long they take to cook will depend on the freshness of your beans, but allow at least 1 hour. Leave them undrained in the pan until you need them.

To make the pasta dough, sift the two flours into a large bowl and add a good pinch of salt. Pour 135 ml (4½ fl oz/generous ½ cup) of the water into the flour, then with firm hands mix the two together to form a dough ball. Use the rest of the water only if you really can't get the dough to form after smooshing and squeezing for a good minute or two. Semolina flour has a tendency to trick novices into thinking one needs more hydration than is necessary, so expect the dough to feel dry until you have worked it for a bit.

When you have formed a pasta ball, place it on your board and knead it for 5 minutes until it is smooth and slightly bouncy. You can use it right away, but if you want to make the bean soup first, place it in a covered bowl to stop it drying out.

Bettina uses a marvellous flat-bottomed reed tray to make the pasta, which one finds across all of southern Italy. A gnocchi board is a good substitute and if you don't have one of those, try the back of a cheese grater; the result is bobbly, not ridged, but it tastes the same.

Cut off a small piece of dough and put the rest back in the bowl to keep it from drying out. Roll the piece of dough into a strand about the thickness and length of a pencil. Cut

Recipe continued next page →

squares of dough from the strand and, using your thumb, press a piece down onto the ridged surface, flattening and rolling it as you go. You'll end up with a curl. Repeat. And get friends and family involved to speed the process up.

To make the soup, heat a good slug of olive oil in a large casserole or Dutch oven over a medium heat and heap in the onion and celery. Give everything a good stir, cover, and cook for about 5 minutes. While the celery and onion are softening, slice up the greens. Pour the passata onto the soffritto and simmer for 20 minutes, then scoop out the cooked beans from their pot and add them, along with the greens. Add some bean water if needed, to keep everything soupy. The bean water can now be discarded. Continue to simmer the mixture for 10 minutes or so until the leaves are tender.

Bring a large saucepan of salted water to the boil and cook the pasta until al dente; this will take about 5 minutes once the water has returned to the boil. Drain the cavatelli, then scoop them into the bean sauce, stir well to combine everything, then serve in hot plates with peperoncino and extra-virgin olive oil poured generously over.

RICE & PULSES

CARLA'S RISI E TOCHI

◆◆◆

CHICKEN STEW RISOTTO FROM VENETO

PREP   3 hours
SERVINGS   4–6

'You know what, you can make a risotto out of anything. It's easy! All the housewives in this area have their own recipes,' said Luigi with a grin. 'We're by the sea which really suits growing Carnaroli rice. It's an old variety; it grows tall which makes it more prone to being damaged by wind and rain. But we prefer it.' 'We' is his family and their *riseria* (rice farm) called La Fagiana, in the Veneto region. La fagiana means 'pheasant' and Luigi says this dish is even better if you swap this with the chicken. 'It's a great dish for autumn, when the fog doesn't leave the fields.' Mum Carla shared her recipe with us. *Risi e tochi* is the local dialect phrase for rice and chicken.

4 tablespoons olive oil
1 x 1.8 kg (4 lb) free-range chicken, jointed into 10 pieces, or 2 hen pheasants
1 tablespoon rosemary needles
1 red onion, diced
1 bay leaf
1 teaspoon salt
150 ml (5 fl oz/scant ⅔ cup) red wine
400 g (14 oz) passata
360 g (12½ oz) Carnaroli rice
simmering water, as needed
75 g (2½ oz) grated Parmigiano Reggiano (or as much as you like)

Heat the oil a casserole or Dutch oven over a medium heat and, when hot, add a few of the chicken pieces – don't overcrowd the casserole or the meat will steam. Brown the chicken pieces in batches, then set to one side. Finely chop the rosemary needles. Add the onion to the casserole with the rosemary, bay leaf and salt and sauté for about 7 minutes until soft but not brown. Deglaze with half of the red wine, let the alcohol evaporate, then return the chicken to the casserole with the passata. Reduce the heat to a medium-low, cover with a lid and simmer until the chicken is cooked, adding water if the sauce starts to catch on the bottom. This should take a good hour. Take the breast pieces out after 30 minutes to stop them from drying out too much; cut them into bite-sized pieces and return them at finishing stage.

Remove the cooked chicken and, when it is cool enough to handle, pull the meat off the bones in chunks. Put to one side, covered with kitchen foil to keep warm. Check the seasoning of the sauce in the casserole, adding more salt if necessary.

Tip the rice into the sauce along with the rest of the wine and give everything a good stir. Keep stirring. Whenever you can see the bottom of the pan as you scrape a wooden spoon through the mixture, add a splash of simmering water. Depending on your rice, the grains will take about 18 minutes to cook. Nibble a couple of grains every few minutes to check for doneness. Carnaroli rice is very forgiving but you don't want mushy risotto.

Stir the chicken through the risotto with the grated Parmigiano. Check the seasoning once again, then serve.

VARIATION   This was an instant hit with my family, and it has evolved! Having cooked a roast chicken, I make a stock with the bones. I use this to make a risotto with whatever wine is to hand, but I think the rosemary is important. I go easy on the passata and stir in leftover bits of roast chicken a couple of minutes before the rice is cooked. I think Carla would approve!

CHECCO'S SBRUFFA BAFFI O MALTAGLIATI ALLA ROMAGNOLA

◆◆◆

DIRTY MOUSTACHES FROM ROMAGNA

PREP	1 hour
SERVINGS	4

FOR THE PASTA

90 g (3 oz/generous ½ cup)
   semolina flour
210 g (7¼ oz/1⅔ cups) 00 flour
145 g (5 oz) egg or 2 eggs
20 g (¾ oz) extra-virgin olive oil
pinch of salt

FOR THE BEAN SOUP

200 ml (7 fl oz/scant 1 cup) extra-
   virgin olive oil, plus extra to serve
1 onion, finely diced
80 ml (2¾ fl oz/⅓ cup)
   dry white wine
300 g (10½ oz) cooked beans
   (or 1 x 400 g/14 oz tin of cannellini
   or borlotti/cranberry beans)
400 g (14 oz) passata
5 g (0.2 oz) salt
1 teaspoon sugar
1 garlic clove
2 tablespoons finely chopped
   flat-leaf parsley

I love it when we find pasta-making grandfathers! Francesco (Checco for short) is a retired school administrator who lives in Faenza. He was the 4th youngest of six boys with a widowed mother who brought her children up to help – and this included making pasta. They developed a routine, Checco explained.

'It was like this: every morning the first one to wake up had to prepare and relight the fire. Then, after breakfast, one dusted and the rest of us made the beds. After that we took it in turns to make the pasta. I guess I was about 9 when I started. My mother always added oil and salt to her dough, so I do too, but it's not usual around here to do that. Mum used what flour there was, but I like to use 30% semolina flour, because it makes a bit firmer pasta for this dish.'

Checco's other talent is crochet, which began when his wife Liu asked for help. The cap he is wearing in his picture is one he made and he has a drawer full of linens and tablecloths. He is currently restoring an antique bedcover for a friend.

Sbruffa baffi is Romagnolo dialect for 'dirty moustaches'. This bean and pasta dish is so called because the random bits of pasta (called *maltagliati* in Italian, meaning 'badly cut') would get caught as hungry workmen slurped them up.

First, make the pasta dough. Weigh the flours and mix them together. Weigh the eggs and scoop a bit out if they are large and weigh a total of more than 145 g (5 oz). Add the oil and mix the two liquids together. Follow the instructions on page 11 for egg pasta dough.

Roll out the dough to a thickness of about 2 mm. If the hydration is good, you won't need extra flour, but sometimes humidity and temperature play fun and games with pasta stickiness, so sprinkle some flour over the surface if it feels a bit sticky. Roll up the sfoglia into a loose log about 3 fingers wide. To cut the *maltagliati* shapes, slice the pasta roll on an angle one way and then another, making sure to create the same sizes, but not necessarily the same shapes. They can be diamonds, triangles or any other shape that takes your fancy, just don't overthink it. Spread them out on the board.

Checco uses an earthenware pot to make this soup because of its gentle cooking, and beans are less prone to sticking. Find a heavy-based saucepan and place it over a medium heat. Pour in a very good slug of olive oil, add the onion and sauté for about 7 minutes until soft and translucent. Deglaze with the white wine.

Recipe continued next page →

Open the tin of beans and place half in the pan. Use a stick blender to purée the beans still in the tin with the liquid. Scrape this into the pan and add the passata, salt and sugar. Give everything a good stir and while this simmers for 10 minutes, crush the garlic clove with a little salt. Add the parsley and garlic just a few minutes before you add the pasta. You will need to stir the beans regularly because they catch and burn on a pan bottom every easily. Don't let it reduce to a sauce – the pasta needs to cook in some liquid.

Dump your pasta into the soup and nibble a piece every minute or so to check for doneness. If it's looking too thick, add a splash of hot water.

Dole out immediately with a generous dose of extra-virgin olive oil over each serving.

ELSA'S RISOTTO CON PORCINI

◆◆◆

PORCINI RISOTTO FROM EMILIA

PREP	1 hour
SERVINGS	4

40 g (1½ oz) dried porcini
1 litre (34 fl oz/4¼ cups)
    good-quality meat stock,
    preferably chicken
100 g (3½ oz) unsalted butter
4 tablespoons olive oil
1 small onion, finely diced (ideally
    as small as the rice grains)
320 g (11¼ oz/2 cups) Arborio
    or Carnaroli risotto rice
a glass of dry white wine (about
    125 ml/4 fl oz/½ cup)
100 g (3½ oz) Parmigiano
    Reggiano, grated, plus extra
    to serve (if you like)
salt

Bar Remo is tucked behind Regent Street; it's the kind of bustling place that has signed autographs on the wall and serves Italian classics like saltimbocca. It's been a family business for over 90 years and Elsa married into it 50-odd years ago. She came to London after the war when she was eight, from a mountain village to the south Piacenza, but her family's connection with London is also a long one. 'My grandpa was an iceman because in those days restaurants didn't have refrigeration. His job was to carry the ice from the wells you can still see behind Kings Cross. And my grandma, well, she walked to London, following the railway lines. To save her shoes she only put them on when she came into a town, because you know – appearances matter!'

'As kids, we had to keep our heads down; memories of the war were still raw, it was understandable. We got a bit bullied and teased, and our mum was always telling us not to speak Italian in public. But we had a strong community. We had our church, we had social clubs – that's how I met Remo – and of course food was a major part of maintaining that family feeling. For some people pasta is comfort food, but for me it's risotto. The great thing about this recipe is that I always have the ingredients in my larder. My dried porcini of course come from my home town!'.

Rinse the dried porcini in cold water, then place them in a small heatproof bowl and cover them with hot water to rehydrate. This will take about 20 minutes. When the mushroom slices are soft, remove them and cut them into small pieces. Save the soaking water for later use.

Pour the meat stock into a saucepan and bring it to a slow simmer.

On the adjacent ring, place a sauté pan over a medium heat and add half of the butter and all the oil (which stops the butter from burning). Once the butter has melted, stir in the onion. Cook for about 7 minutes until it is translucent – don't let it brown – then add the chopped porcini and fry for another few minutes to soften the porcini further.

Add the rice to the pan and stir to toast for a couple of minutes until the grains are translucent. They should sound gritty.

Deglaze with the white wine – Elsa always sneaks a glass from her husband's bottle – and, when the alcohol has evaporated, add a pinch of salt and a couple of ladlefuls of hot stock followed by the porcini soaking water, using a tea strainer to strain the porcini water into the pan as it can be gritty. Keep stirring and adding stock whenever you can part the rice with a spoon. When the rice is firm but not crunchy, turn off the heat, add the rest of the butter and the grated cheese, and stir well. Cover the pan and let the risotto rest for 5 minutes before serving on warm plates, with more grated Parmigiano if you wish.

GIULINA'S RISI E BISI

◆◆◆

RICE AND PEAS FROM VENETO

PREP	1 hour
SERVINGS	4

1 kg (2 lb 4 oz) peas in the pods,
   or 600 g (1 lb 5 oz) frozen peas
6 tablespoons extra-virgin olive oil
1 onion, finely diced
320 g (11¼ oz/scant 2 cups) risotto
   rice, preferably Vialone Nano
4 heaped tablespoons finely
   chopped parsley
40 g (1½ oz) unsalted butter
60 g (2 oz) Parmigiano Reggiano,
   grated
salt
black pepper (optional)

Giulina's name was a misspelling of Giulia by the registrar in charge of recording births in Venice. She has kept the erroneous 'n' for the fun of it. Before she retired, she had a career catering for the primary school children of Venice; apparently her pasta and beans was a favourite. But she is also famous for her *risi e bisi,* or rice and peas, a dish which is typical of the Veneto region.

She lives in Murano, an island just a short ferry ride from Venice; tourists flock there for its glass blowing, but devoted vegetable lovers get off at the next stop, the lesser-known island of Sant'Erasmo. It is a small, crocheted vegetative blanket of market gardening, laden with produce and struggling to stay afloat in the lagoon. It's where Giulina sources her organic peas; she thinks organically-grown ones are essential because you want to make a stock from the pods. This makes it a seasonal treat!

We spent a jolly afternoon with Giulina and her friends who dropped by, discovering Venetian women are welcoming, earthy, love a good laugh and the chance to celebrate. So we all had a glass of wine and within minutes, it was a risi e bisi impromptu party.

If you're using peas in pods, shell the peas and place the pods in a saucepan with plenty of water. Cover and simmer gently for about 1 hour until they're very soft. Alternatively, use a pressure cooker to speed up the process. Scoop out the pods and pass them through a food mill, scraping the resulting purée back into the water to create the stock. Season with salt to taste and keep warm in a saucepan over a low heat.

If you don't have access to fresh peas, you can use frozen ones instead. Place 1.2 litres (40 fl oz/5 cups) of water with 300 g (10½ oz) of peas into a saucepan and bring them to the boil with 4 g – 2 heavy pinches – of salt. Cover the pan and cook the peas for 8 minutes. Strain them, allow them to cool for 2 minutes, then purée until very smooth.

Heat the olive oil in a sauté pan over a medium heat, add the onion with a pinch of salt and cook for 5–7 minutes until softened but not browned. Add the rice and the remaining fresh peas: how many is up to you. Sauté the mixture for a few minutes until the grains are semi-translucent. Add half the parsley; keep frying, season with salt, then start adding in the stock 2 ladlefuls at a time. Add more stock when the rice starts to dry out. If you are using frozen peas, add them now.

You're aiming for a sloppy risotto. Once the rice is cooked – it should be al dente but not chalky in the middle – take the pan off the heat and stir in the rest of the parsley, the butter and Parmigiano. Let it rest, covered, for 3–5 minutes; if it thickens up too much, stir in a little more stock. Serve with more cheese and some black pepper if you like.

LICIA'S PASTA TIRASÚ O TAJAÍN CON FAGIOLI E CAVOLO

◆◆◆

TAGLIATELLE WITH CABBAGE AND BEANS FROM CINQUE TERRE

PREP	2 hours, plus overnight soaking
SERVINGS	6
DRIED PASTA ALTERNATIVE	Tagliatelle

Peer cautiously over 89-year-old Licia's balcony; there's a 30-metre drop before the land tumbles into the sea. She has a grandstand view of the waves breaking onto the Cinque Terre coastline from every window. 'I've spent 70 years looking at this view and I never tire of it. I think gazing into all that light is why I had a little cancer in one eye.' Licia laughed – it's a price worth paying for the daily spangled splendour whatever the weather.

Licia's family were farmers who produced a little bit of everything, including wine. Not having an older brother, Licia's jobs as a youngster included mending the vine supports, which is harder than it sounds as vineyards in Cinque Terre are steeply terraced. Fertiliser for the vines was sheep manure; when Licia had pruned the vines, she'd take the trimmings to use them as bedding for her mother's rather wild, horned sheep. 'The dry stone walls that keep the soils in place needed regular maintenance too, but that was the one thing I didn't have to do. Otherwise, I worked as a man. It was normal that you earned nothing, but you worked very hard.' And the wine? 'Dad's production was 1,500 litres a year and it was sold in an instant!'

Licia calls this pasta several names. *Tajaín* is the local name for tagliatelle and *pasta tirasú* is from the Italian *'tirata su'*, meaning pulled up. Licia explained: 'There is a saying – "*quando il fumo va al camino tira su i tajaín*" – that means that as soon as they are boiling they have to be pulled out.'

The use of *semola rimacinata* (semolina flour) is unusual in Liguria, but Licia's mother discovered it during the war while searching for food and groceries. 'I think it makes great pasta,' Licia says. 'It works really well with these vegetables.'

This dish is based on using what is growing in your veg garden. In winter, Licia uses cavolo nero; in spring, she prefers a local cabbage called lavagnino; you could use spring greens, collards, savoy cabbage, anything with robust green leaves.

FOR THE PASTA
300 g (10½ oz/2½ cups) semolina flour
145 ml (5 fl oz/⅔ cup) warm water

Start with the soup base. Drain the beans and place them in a saucepan with fresh water and ½ a teaspoon of salt. Let them simmer gently for about 1 hour. Licia does not add anything else to the cooking liquid, which works fine if your beans and veggies are top notch and bursting with flavour thanks to Ligurian soil and sunshine. If in any doubt, add a bay leaf and whole garlic clove to the cooking water and remove them before you add the veggies.

Recipe continued next page →

FOR THE SOUP

300 g (10½ oz) dried borlotti
  (cranberry) beans, rinsed and
  soaked in cold water overnight
  with 1 teaspoon salt
300 g (10½ oz) cavolo nero
  or other robust greens
2 large potatoes, peeled and cut
  into bite-sized chunks
sea salt

TO SERVE

grated Parmigiano Reggiano
extra-virgin olive oil
  (try and find good quality)

Rinse the cavolo nero then use a knife to cut along each side of the tough spines to remove them. Roll up the leaves and slice across it to create thick crinkly ribbons. Add the cavolo nero and potatoes to the beans, adding more water so that they are covered, and adjust the seasoning. Make sure the mixture continues to simmer.

Make the pasta dough as described on page 13. Leave it to rest, covered, for 30 minutes, then use a rolling pin to roll it out to a thickness of 2 mm. Let it dry for 10 minutes on your board before rolling up like a carpet into a 3-finger-wide loose roll. Cut it into 5 mm (¼ in)-wide strips.

Heap the pasta strips directly into the soup, give it a good stir. Pasta cooked with other things like this always takes longer, so contrary to the saying above, leave it to simmer for 4–5 minutes before checking the pasta is done. There's no need to drain anything here, just dole it out into warmed soup bowls.

Dress each serving with generous amounts of grated Parmigiano and a good slug of extra-virgin olive oil poured over the top. Ideally, drink white wine from Licia's family vineyard, Cantina Crovara, which is now run by her beloved nephew Alessandro.

LINA'S STRICCHETTI CON PISELLI E SALSICCE

♦♦♦

BUTTERFLY PASTA WITH PEAS AND SAUSAGE FROM ROMAGNA

PREP	2 hours
SERVINGS	8
DRY PASTA ALTERNATIVE	Farfalle

Eighty-seven-year-old Lina, like a lot of the women we film, continues to keep a vegetable garden and chickens; habits gained through necessity die hard. She was the youngest daughter of four children. Her mum gave her bits of pasta dough to play with and by the time she was ten years old she was making pasta regularly. 'She'd give me some flour and eggs and then it was up to me. To begin with, I couldn't even reach the pasta board! Of course my mum and aunts laughed when I made holes in the pasta. They said don't worry you'll do better next time. But my daughters aren't interested, though a partner of one of them likes to make it with me when he comes over.'

This egg pasta uses the usual 1 egg for every 100 g (3½ oz) of flour, but – growing up – this wasn't the case for Lina. She would perhaps use one egg and make up the rest of the liquid with water. Eggs could be bartered for the other things the family needed like oil and sugar.

This recipe is a family favourite. When Lina's husband was alive, he kept a couple of pigs and so the sausages were homemade. Now she relies on her local butcher, but she continues to grow her own peas, which she freezes for year-round use; something not possible in her youth.

Be careful not to over-season the sauce. Between the sausages and the Parmigiano used to finish the dish, you may not need to add very much (if any at all). It's best to let the sauce rest for 4 hours or more, as this will blend and improve the flavours. 'Often in Italy, we make a sauce like this in advance and use it at the end of, or the next, day.'

FOR THE PASTA

500 g (1 lb 2 oz/4¼ cups) 00 flour
275g (9¾ oz) egg or 5 eggs

FOR THE SAUCE

200 g (7 oz) onion
100 g (3½ oz) carrot
100 g (3½ oz) celery stalks
60 ml (2 fl oz/4 tablespoons) olive oil
pinch of salt
300–350 g (10½–12 oz) Italian
 pork sausages
100 ml (3½ fl oz/scant ½ cup)
 dry white wine
400 g (14 oz) passata
250 g (9 oz) green peas
freshly ground black pepper

Make the egg pasta dough as described on page 11. Let it rest, covered, for at least 30 minutes; it's better if you can wait 45–60 minutes so it can relax even more for easy rolling out. Make a pasta sheet about 1 mm thick. Using a pastry cutter, cut 3 cm (1¼ in)-wide strips, then cut diagonally across each ribbon to make longish diamond shapes. Pick up a piece, holding it vertically. Fold the left corner under the middle and the right corner over the middle to make a zigzag in the centre and pinch hard to make them stick. You should have what looks like a butterfly or bowtie shape. Check out her video to watch Lina make them.

TO SERVE

20 g (¾ oz) grated Parmigiano
 Reggiano per person

Recipe continued next page →

Recipe continued →

While the pasta is resting, make a soffritto by either dicing the onion, carrot and celery into tiny pieces about the size of a rice grain, or do as Lina does and use a food processor to pulse-chop the vegetables.

Warm up the olive oil in a large sauté pan over a medium heat, then add your soffritto with a pinch of salt. Fry gently for about 10 minutes until it has softened and you cannot discern the aroma of the individual cooking vegetables.

Remove the casing from the sausages and crumble the meat with your fingers. Stir this through the soffritto, breaking up the large bits into smaller crumbles with a spoon. Keep stirring and crumbling for about 5 minutes until the meat is no longer red (browning the meat isn't necessary). This process is called *sbianchire* in Italian. It means 'to make it white' – even though the meat goes a kind of grey beige! Add the wine and continue to stir, letting the alcohol evaporate. You will know when it has evaporated by wafting the air from the pan up to your nose with your hand; you shouldn't be able to smell it or have the faint acid 'tingle' as you inhale. Pour in the passata and stir all ingredients together well. Leave it to simmer for a couple of minutes then check for seasoning. It probably won't need salt, but it could do with a bit of pepper.

Fresh peas usually take longer to cook than frozen, so add them now. If your peas are frozen, let the sauce simmer for about 10 minutes before you add them to the mix. If necessary, add a splash of water to make sure the meat is just covered by liquid at the beginning of cooking. The sauce should simmer for about 15 minutes.

In the meantime, bring a large pot of salted water to the boil. When the water is boiling, drop in your pasta. If the pasta is very fresh it might take only 30 seconds–1 minute. If you made it well in advance and you left it to dry, taste the pasta every minute or so to know when it is done to your liking.

To finish the dish, strain the pasta and add it to the sauté pan with the heated sauce. Gently sauté and toss the two elements together.

Plate your pasta and sauce, adding a sprinkle of Parmigiano and a bit more pepper on top. Serve warm. Never add cheese to the hot sauce pan unless you have experience, it will just clump and stick. If you want to be Italian, do not wait to eat fresh pasta, especially if you are in a big group!

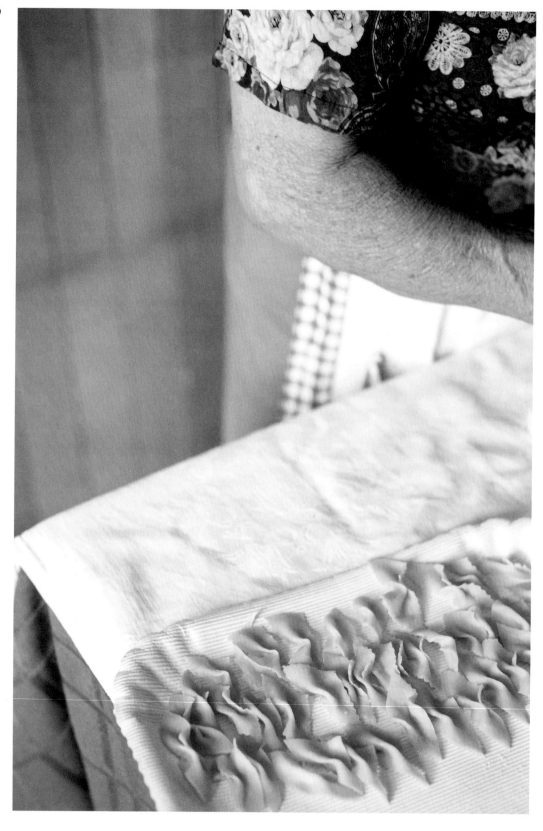

MARIA ROSA'S PANISSA

♦♦♦

RUSTIC SAUSAGE AND BEAN RISOTTO FROM VERCELLI

PREP	3 hours, plus 12 hours soaking time
SERVINGS	4

The landscape between Milan and Turin is green-quilted and water-stitched for much of the year. Tucked into the seams are hamlets with small houses and large rice barns against which rusting metal tractor wheels lean, abandoned. Maria Rosa's village boasts a butcher who makes a fresh salami called salami della duia, which is made with garlic and red wine; it is pretty much impossible to find this salami anywhere else in Italy. And the borlotti (cranberry) beans are a variety unique to the Vercelli area called fagioli di Saluggia. Thus, this recipe is not authentic because I had to swap these ingredients for ones more generally available. It tastes very similar, however, and is delicious.

Maria said that this is an end of harvest festival dish which would send workers away with full tummies and smiling faces. In her youth she was a *mondina*, a rice worker, and one of her responsibilities was making panissa for everyone.

FOR THE PORK STOCK

1 celery stalk, chopped
1 onion, chopped
1 carrot, chopped
500 g (1 lb 2 oz) pork ribs
1 pork trotter, or 200 g (7 oz) pork ribs if you can't find a trotter
1 bay leaf
10 black peppercorns, cracked

FOR THE PANISSA

100 g (3½ oz/½ cup) dried borlotti (cranberry) beans, soaked in water for 12 hours
1 small onion, finely diced (ideally as small as the rice grains)
250 g (9 oz) best-quality fresh-range pork sausage meat
100 g (3½ oz) salami, finely chopped with 1 garlic clove
320 g (11¼ oz/scant 1½ cups) Carnaroli rice
100 ml (3½ fl oz/scant ½ cup) Barbera red wine
100 g (3½ oz) passata
1.5 litres (50 fl oz/6¼ cups) pork stock (above)
grated Grana Padano or Parmigiano Reggiano, to serve
salt

Put 3 litres (102 fl oz/12¾ cups) of water in a stock pot. Chop the vegetables and add these to the water along with the bones, bay leaf and peppercorns. Bring the mixture quickly to the boil then reduce the heat and let everything simmer for about 2 hours. Taste the liquid: if you have used a trotter, the stock may need to simmer a little longer to achieve the best flavour.

Strain the stock through a fine sieve, discard the solids, then return the stock to the pot. Drain the beans and add them to the stock; return it to a simmer. Cook for about 1 hour – the beans' cooking time will depend on their freshness. Add a teaspoon of salt after the first 20 minutes of cooking.

Scoop the cooked beans from the stock and set aside. Keep the stock simmering while you prep the rice.

Heat a sauté pan over a medium heat and add the onion and meats, breaking up the sausage meat if necessary. You won't need to add any oil as the meat will render enough fat to cook the onion.

Once the onion is translucent and the meat no longer pink, add the rice and keep stirring for a couple of minutes; because of the meat the rice will not toast like in a classic risotto recipe, but it will soak up the flavourful juices. Pour in the red wine and let the alcohol evaporate (you can smell when the alcohol is no longer there) then add the tomato passata. When the rice has absorbed the liquids, start adding the simmering stock, a few ladlefuls at a time. Adjust the seasoning and keep cooking and adding stock for about 18 minutes (check the rice cooking time on the packet) until the rice is cooked. Stir through the cooked borlotti beans.

Serve hot, with plenty of grated Parmigiano stirred through it.

NINNI'S ARANCINI

♦♦♦

SICILIAN DEEP-FRIED RICE BALLS

PREP	3 hours plus overnight resting
SERVINGS	8

Ninni lives near Catania in Sicily where arancini are large and pointed (and the spelling is with an 'i'; on the western side of the island, they are arancine). Ninni says they are meant to resemble Mount Etna and the oozy filling looks like lava.

She works in the local butchers and makes arancini for church festivals where, of course, they are hugely popular. There are multiple stages in this recipe, and the trickiest bit is stopping people from eating them as they come out of the fryer. Use Arborio rice for this recipe because of its starchiness, which helps the grains stick together.

If you cannot find caciocavallo, use any cheese that's good for melting, such as fior di latte (cow's milk mozzarella).

100 g (3½ oz) caciocavallo cheese, or other good cheese for melting
2 eggs, beaten
200 g (7 oz) fine dry breadcrumbs
2 litres (68 fl oz/8½ cups) peanut oil, for frying
salt and pepper

FOR THE RICE

500 g (1 lb 2 oz/4 cups) arborio rice
about 1 litre (34 fl oz/4¼ cups) vegetable stock
a good pinch of ground saffron
60 g (2 oz) butter

FOR THE RAGÙ

1 onion (about 150 g/5 oz)
1 celery stalk (about 100 g/3½ oz)
1 carrot (about 100 g/3½ oz)
1 tablespoon olive oil
300 g (10½ oz) minced (ground) pork
1 tablespoon tomato concentrate
120 ml (4 fl oz/½ cup) dry white wine
700 g (1 lb 9 oz) passata
200 g (7 oz) green peas (frozen are fine)

FOR THE BÉCHAMEL

20 g (¾ oz) unsalted butter
25 g (1 oz) 0 flour
250 ml (8 fl oz/1 cup) cold full-fat milk
pinch of grated nutmeg

Weigh the rice, then measure twice its volume in stock. This volume method ensures all the stock will be absorbed. Bring the stock to a rolling boil in a saucepan and season with 1 teaspoon of salt. Add the rice and the saffron and cook, stirring occasionally, until all the liquid has been absorbed and the rice is al dente. Depending on how wide and shallow your pan is, you might need a little extra stock to complete the cooking of the rice. Take the pan off the heat and, while the rice is still very hot, briskly stir in the butter. Let it cool for several hours until it is completely cold. You can also leave it overnight in a covered container in the refrigerator. Once cold, taste and check the seasoning; you want it properly salted otherwise the end result will be bland.

Now make the ragù. Large chunks of onion or celery will make your arancini fall apart, so blitz the onion, carrot and celery in a food processor until finely chopped. Heat the oil in a frying pan over a medium heat, add the onion and fry for a couple of minutes until slightly softened, then add the veggie mixture with a pinch of salt. Gently sauté everything for about 7 minutes until the onion is translucent and soft. Add the pork and tomato paste and stir until the meat is no longer pink. Pour in the wine and wait until the alcohol has evaporated before stirring in the passata. Taste and adjust the salt and pepper seasoning, then let the sauce simmer gently for about 30 minutes. You want the liquid to have reduced so that you can see the bottom of the pan when you drag a spoon through it. Add the peas and simmer until they are cooked.

Recipe continued next page →   **RICE & PULSES**

Let the ragù cool completely before using it for arancini. This quantity is more then you need for arancini, but it's the minimum amount for making a decently-flavoured sauce. Use the leftovers for pasta dishes.

To make the béchamel sauce, heat a small non-stick saucepan over a medium-low heat, add the butter and let it melt, then add the flour and whisk for a minute or so until well blended but not coloured. Gradually add the cold milk and keep whisking until the sauce has thickened and is smooth. Season with salt, pepper and nutmeg. Taste to make sure the raw flour flavour is gone. Let it cool completely.

So now you have three cold mixtures. Before you start playing with the arancini, cut the cheese into batons about 10–12 g (¼ oz) in weight and 6 cm (2½ in) long.

Mix 8 tablespoons of the ragù and 4 tablespoons of the béchamel sauce to begin with. You might need a little more, in which case mix in a 2:1 meat-to-sauce ratio.

Place the eggs in a shallow dish with 2 pinches of salt and whisk them thoroughly with a fork so that when you lift it up, the eggs drain evenly through the prongs. Place the breadcrumbs on a plate. Now you are ready to form arancini!

Cover the palm of one hand with rice about 1 cm (½ in) thick. Use your other hand to add a cheese baton and a tablespoon of the sauce, then take a palmful of rice in your other hand and close it over the other hand as you could in prayer. Mould and pat it to make a pointed cone shape. They're meant to be large. Once you have formed an arancino, dip it completely in the egg wash, then remove any excess egg by letting it drip a bit before rolling it in the breadcrumbs.

Place each one, pointed side up, on a tray. Refrigerate for 30 minutes while you heat the oil. Make sure you have a cooking thermometer.

Find a tall pot and fill it with the peanut oil. This should be enough for the arancini to be completely submerged when you first add one to the oil. Heat the oil to 160–170°C (325–338°F).

With the help of a spider skimmer, carefully transfer an arancino to the hot oil, being sure to not splash yourself or overcrowd the pot – cooking two at a time is a good idea. Fry them for about 10 minutes, turning them regularly until golden brown. They will bob to the surface as they cook. Transfer the cooked arancini to kitchen paper to drain. Eat warm or cold, but not hot.

SARINA'S LOLLI CON LE FAVE

✦✦✦

CAVATELLI PASTA WITH BROAD BEANS AND DANDELIONS FROM MODICA

PREP	1 hour, plus resting time
SERVINGS	6

FOR THE BEANS

400 g (14 oz) dried whole broad
    beans, skin on
1 teaspoon bicarbonate of soda
    (baking soda)
1 bay leaf
1 onion, peeled and quartered
500 g (1 lb 2 oz) dandelion leaves

FOR THE PASTA

400 g (14 oz/3⅓ cups)
    semolina flour
200 ml (7 fl oz/scant 1 cup)
    warm water
6 g (0.2 oz) salt

TO SERVE

peperoncino flakes
Sicilian extra-virgin olive oil

Farmer Sarina rears Charolais beef cattle near Modica in Sicily. She explains, 'I grew up with cows, then when I got married at 18 we began to keep some, and I learned to milk them. I do other work too, like harvesting olives, almonds and carob.'

She's a busy woman, who still finds the time to make this pasta everyday for her husband. Sarina is in fact continuing a local tradition. The Modica Cottoia broad bean was used to feed livestock and rotated with other crops, and so farm labourers were given a daily ration to eat. They are very easy to cook; hence its name *cottoia* – or 'fast cooking' in the local dialect. In fact, this dish is a double dose of easy; the pasta name lolli comes from the word *lollo*, which means 'silly' in the local dialect.

'I plant the beans in November and harvest them in May. As for the lolli, I watched my grandmother and mum making them from a very young age. They taught me. Now I make them for my husband. He gets pasta and beans nearly every day of the year. The greens vary through the year; now I use dandelions.' Dandelions are earthy and bitter; the younger the leaves are less so, and the season for them is very early spring before they start flowering. Choose a kale or cabbage if you don't want to go foraging.

The night before you want to cook the beans, place them in plenty of cold water with the bicarbonate of soda. This helps to soften the skin. The next day, drain the water, rinse the beans and put them in a saucepan, cover them with water and bring them to the boil. Cook them for 15 minutes, then drain them. Once cool enough to handle, remove the hilum (the black part of the bean skin from each bean) – it's pretty hard and inedible, but if you don't mind that, you can skip this step!

Return the beans to the saucepan. Cover with at least 5 cm (2 in) of water and add the bay leaf. Plop in the pieces of onion in along with a pinch of salt and simmer for a good hour, topping up with water if need be.

Give your dandelion greens a good wash and trim all the tough woody bits at the base of the stem. Tear the leaves in half and add them to the beans halfway through cooking.

Make the pasta dough as described on page 13. Cut off a chunk of dough and roll it out to form a rope the thickness of a breadstick. Cut it into 7 cm (2¾ in) lengths, long enough to accommodate 5 fingers (you'll need both hands for rolling). Repeat this process until you've used up all the dough. Take a length and place 5 fingers along it. Press down and pull it towards you; you'll create a dimply hollow in the pasta. Repeat, spreading the lolli out on a towel or board to dry a little.

When the beans are just about done, check the liquid levels. You need enough bean broth to cook the pasta properly but so the final result is a thick, chunky stew. If necessary, add some water and bring it back to the simmer before adding the pasta. The lolli will need about 5 minutes to cook.

Ladle this into pasta bowls and sprinkle with peperoncino flakes and a good dose of Sicilian extra-virgin olive oil.

four

meat & seafood

ADI'S ANELLETTI AL FORNO ALLA PALERMITANA

❖❖❖

BAKED PASTA FROM PALERMO

PREP	2 hours
SERVINGS	8

DRY PASTA ALTERNATIVE	about 500 g (1 lb 2 oz) boxed anelletti pasta

FOR THE ANELLETTI

400 g (14 oz/3⅓ cups)
  semolina flour
185–200 ml (6½–7 fl oz)
  warm water
a pinch of salt

FOR THE RAGÙ

4 tablespoons olive oil
1 onion, finely diced
2 carrots, 1 finely diced, 1 whole
2 celery sticks, finely diced
1 tablespoon tomato concentrate
300 g (10½ oz) each of minced
  (ground) pork and beef
3 cloves
1 kg (2 lb 4 oz) passata
150 g (5 oz) green peas
salt and pepper

FOR THE TIMBALLO

2 or 3 aubergines (eggplants)
plenty of olive oil or vegetable oil,
  for frying
butter, for greasing the pan
50 g (1¾ oz) fine dry breadcrumbs
200 g (7 oz) grated caciocavallo
  or provolone cheese
200 g (7 oz) primo sale cheese,
  cubed (fresh, not-too-salty feta
  is a good substitute)

Farmer Emmanuela breeds pedigree cows, produces a dried pasta range using heritage durum wheat, and runs an agriturismo called Masseria Acque di Palermo. 'You must film my mother's timballo!' she declared, when she found out about Pasta Grannies. Her mother, Adi, was way too gracious a host to be startled by a film crew appearing on her doorstep the next morning to shoot Palermo's classic Sunday-lunch dish. Tiny hooped pasta (*anelletti*) is essential; if you are keen you can make them, otherwise buy them like most cooks do.

If you are making your own anelletti, make the pasta dough as described on page 13 and knead it for 5 minutes until it's smooth and has a light bounce. Cover the dough ball with reusable plastic or a damp cloth and leave it at room temperature for 20 minutes to let it rehydrate completely; it should be tacky to the touch when taken out to form anelletti.

Cut off a small piece of dough and keep the rest covered so it doesn't dry out. Roll the piece out to a thin string, ideally 2 mm in diameter. Wrap this string around your forefinger. Snip the strand with your thumbnail against the finger making sure the two ends overlap a bit and then press and roll the two ends together with your forefinger and thumb gently until you get a little circle. Repeat. When rolling strands, it's useful to have spray bottle of water to spritz your hands – you want them a bit tacky but not wet; this helps to apply the moisture to the strand and gives you a better 'grip'. Don't be tempted to roll out long strands – the pasta will dry out and become difficult to roll.

To make the ragù, heat the 4 tablespoons of olive oil in a large sauté pan, add the finely diced onion, carrot and celery and fry gently for 10 minutes until soft but not coloured. Stir through the tomato concentrate, season with a teaspoon of salt, then add the meat and keep stirring until the latter is no longer pink.

Punch the 3 cloves into the second carrot and add this along with the passata, then simmer everything for a good 45 minutes until the meat is fully cooked and there's a nice oily surface to the sauce. Remove the clove-carrot. Stir in the peas and continue to cook for 2–3 minutes until the peas are soft but not mushy.

Half-cook the fresh or shop-bought anelletti (they continue cooking in the oven and you don't want mushy pasta), then drain well and put to one side while you prep the aubergines. You may need all three, depending on how big they are to begin with.

Pour enough oil into a non-stick sauté pan to cover the base. Heat the oil over a medium-high heat until the oil starts to shimmer. Cut one aubergine into 2 cm (¾ in) cubes and season with fine salt. Fry the cubes for about 5 minutes, in batches if necessary – you want them to fry, not stew. They are ready when they have started to turn brown and have gone a bit soft.

Slice the other aubergine lengthways, making slipper shapes about 1 cm (½ in) thick. Season the slices with salt and fry them in more oil; they are cooked when they bend easily.

Grease the inside of a 23 x 8 cm (9 x 3 in) deep springform cake tin with butter, then sprinkle it generously with breadcrumbs. Arrange the aubergine slices to cover the bottom and sides, making sure they overlap a bit. Keep three slices for the top.

Mix the cooked pasta with the ragù; you may not need all the ragù, but make sure the pasta is heavily dressed as it will absorb more liquid during baking. Stir through the grated cheeses, the cubed cheese and the cooked aubergine cubes. Taste and adjust seasoning, then pour the pasta mixture into the tin. Next, you need to create an aubergine case by laying more aubergine slices across the top of the pasta, then folding over the side slices. Don't leave any gaps.

Brush the top with some oil or melted butter and sprinkle some more breadcrumbs over the top.

Bake the timballo in the oven for about 50 minutes; be prepared to let it cook a little bit longer if it's not golden brown enough. Remove it from the oven and let it cool for 20 minutes at room temperature before removing the timballo from its tin.

ANNA MARIA'S ZITI ALLA GENOVESE

♦♦♦

PASTA WITH STEWED BEEF FROM NAPLES

PREP 30 minutes,
plus 2½ hours braising

SERVINGS 4–6

FOR THE PASTA
400 g (14 oz) ziti or other dry
pasta such as penne, paccheri,
rigatoni

FOR THE SAUCE
extra-virgin olive oil
600 g (1 lb 5 oz) stewing beef,
cut into 5 cm (2 in) chunks
1 kg (2 lb 4 oz) or 4 large
red onions, thinly sliced
1 carrot, thinly sliced
1 celery stick, thinly sliced
1 bay leaf
100 ml (3½ fl oz/scant ½ cup)
dry white wine
water or beef stock, as required
salt

TO SERVE
grated pecorino
black pepper

I am often asked how we find our grandmothers, and the answer is: we ask everyone – from mayors to hotel receptionists – if they can suggest a *nonna*. In this case, the Pasta Grannies team were staying in a rented apartment in Naples and the host's mum, Anna Maria, turned out to be a Pasta Granny. This recipe of Anna's is a typical Sunday lunch for Neapolitans.

'Think of the sauce as onions with meat,' Anna Maria explained. 'And the onions are important. Ideally they should be the Montoro variety (grown in the Avellino area of Campania) or the Tropea onion. These are fragrant red onions. And you must select beef cuts which you can cook for hours.' Here is her recipe, cooked against a backdrop of a ruined temple, surrounded and hidden by worse-for-wear blocks of flats.

Pour a slug of olive oil into a large casserole dish (in the old days it would have been earthenware, which is better for a gentle braise). Heat this over a medium heat for a couple of minutes then start browning the beef a few pieces at a time. Once all the beef pieces have a bit of colour, return them to the pan along with the vegetables. Season with salt, drop in the bay leaf, give everything a good stir and pour in the wine. Cover and braise the vegetables and meat for about 3 hours. Check the mixture regularly and if it starts to stick, add a little water or beef stock. What you are aiming for is a creamy onion sauce, and beef so soft you can cut it with a fork. Shred the meat if you like, or alternatively remove it to serve as a second course.

Ziti are long, so break them in half. Bring a large saucepan of salted water to the boil and cook the pasta for the time stated on the packet. Drain the pasta thoroughly. Place it in a large bowl and mix it well with the onion and beef sauce.

Let everyone add their own cheese and pepper if they like it.

And PS: No-one knows why a pasta dish from Naples is named after the city of Genova. There are lots of theories; for example, there were lots of Genovese chefs working in Naples in the 15th century.

BENEDETTA'S CASSATELLE A SPIGA

◆◆◆

RICOTTA DUMPLINGS IN FISH BROTH FROM TRAPANI

PREP	2 hours
SERVINGS	6 (makes 18 pieces)

Benedetta is passionate about preserving and promoting local culinary traditions in her home town of Trapani, Sicily. She is an active member of Associazione Cucina Siciliana, which organises demonstrations and classes in the area and this is how we found out about cassatelle a spiga; pleated dumplings filled with a sweetened ricotta and poached in fish stock. The name translates as 'ears of wheat'. Like the similar-shaped culurgiones from Sardinia, they are a bit of a fiddle, but making these is a good group activity.

Benedetta has a close relationship with her local fishermen and had bought a selection of small bony fish direct from the boats on the day we filmed her. They included scorpion fish, weever fish and red mullet. You will need to adjust the fish combination depending on where in the world you are, but I recommend you do not use oily fish like salmon, or blue fish like mackerel or bonito, as the flavour is too strong. Use crustacea like shrimp for a flavour boost. Your fishmonger may be able to supply fish bones; in which case chop them roughly and add them with the onions. If your fish are large, discard their heads as these can give a cloudy appearance to the stock.

And if fresh fish are tricky to find, Benedetta says that at Easter cassatelle a spiga are also poached in a chicken stock.

FOR THE FISH STOCK

60 ml (2 fl oz/4 tablespoons) extra-virgin olive oil
1 onion, sliced
4 ripe, large tomatoes or a 400 g (14 oz) tin good-quality cherry tomatoes
20 g (¾ oz) flat-leaf parsley, roughly chopped
1 litre (34 fl oz/4¼ cups) water (plus extra if necessary)
500 g (1 lb 2 oz) bony small fish
salt

FOR THE GARLIC PESTO

15 g (½ oz) almonds, chopped
3 medium garlic cloves, chopped
generous pinch of rock salt
2 tablespoons extra-virgin olive oil

FOR THE FILLING

500 g (1 lb 2 oz) sheep's milk ricotta
grated zest of 1 large organic lemon (unwaxed)
1 tablespoon caster (superfine) sugar

To make the fish stock, put the oil and onion in a large stock pot and place over a medium heat. Stir well, add a pinch of salt and let the onion soften without caramelising – this will take about 7 minutes. Chop up the fresh tomatoes, if using, keeping the juice. Stir the fresh or tinned tomatoes and parsley into the softened onion and fry gently for another 3–4 minutes, before pouring in the water. Let everything simmer for 10 minutes.

While the water simmers, make the pesto. Put the almonds, garlic and rock salt in a mortar and use the pestle to muddle and pound everything to a paste, then gradually add the oil; it won't emulsify easily if you add it all at once.

Add the pesto and the fish to the stock pot; if the fish aren't completely submerged, add a little more boiling water. Simmer gently for 30 minutes, then strain through a fine-mesh sieve and reserve. If you are a 'get ahead' kind of cook, you can keep the stock refrigerated for 24 hours without significant loss of flavour. If you want to keep it any longer than this, it should be put in the freezer and used within 1 month.

Now make the filling. Sheep's milk ricotta has more flavour than cow's, but the downside is it's more watery, so put it in a sieve and drain it over a bowl for a couple of hours before using a fork to combine it with the other ingredients. Keep it refrigerated while you make the pasta.

FOR THE PASTA

200 g (7 oz/1⅔ cups)
semolina flour
90 ml (3 fl oz) water

Mix the flour and water in a large bowl. You'll need to squish it a bit to form a solid ball of dough. Make sure all the flour is incorporated, then turn it out onto a wooden board and knead it for 2 minutes. If it is dry or crumbly at this stage, wet your hands and keep kneading for a good 8–10 minutes. You are aiming for a smooth, elastic texture which is important if you are going to pleat the *cassatelle* successfully. Set a timer!

Recipe continued next page →

Recipe continued →

A thick sfoglia will result in hefty, stodgy cassatelle, thus you need to roll out the dough to a thickness of 1 mm. Benedetta uses a pasta-rolling machine to do this, so you can too if you like.

Using a 10 cm (4 in) pastry cutter or an upside-down glass of the same diameter, cut out pasta discs. Try to stamp them close together to minimise the offcuts.

If you find yourself with lots of excess bits and pieces, mould them together and only knead the pasta until you have an even ball of dough. If you keep on kneading it, your pasta will end up a bit rubbery and difficult to work with. Keep the dough covered until you can roll it out and make more cassatelle. Only re-knead the dough once. Any further leftovers can be cut up into odd shape pieces – which Italians call maltagliate – and used in (another) soup.

Place a large tablespoon (25–30 g/1 oz) of filling into the centre of a pasta disc. Cup it as you would a taco shell and with the other hand pinch the edges from one side to another to form what looks like a braid. Don't lose touch with the pasta, it's a continuous process. There may be a bit of excess filling as you reach the end; wipe it away. Twist the end pleat so it won't open during cooking. It's best if you refer back to Benedetta's video to get a good idea of how to do it. Remember, if you fail to achieve a pretty pleat, it will still taste the same.

Bring the strained stock to a simmer in a saucepan, then check and adjust the salt seasoning. Use a slotted spoon to lower your cassatelle into the stock. The cooking time will depend on the thickness you have achieved with your pasta, and the folds take longer to cook. Allow 7 minutes to begin with. Place three cassatelle in a soup bowl and ladle over the stock.

BIGGINA'S FETTUCCINE CON CONIGLIO ALL'ISCHITANA

♦♦♦

FETTUCCINE WITH BRAISED RABBIT FROM ISCHIA

PREP	2 hours, plus resting
SERVINGS	4–6
DRIED PASTA ALTERNATIVE	Bucatini

Biggina was the youngest of nine children. Her first job on her parents' small farm began was to move the rotted manure to the vegetables using a basket on her head. She did this after school in the mornings. At school, she loved history: 'I loved the stories and the drama, even though my teacher was a fascist and only wanted to talk about certain events.' She was able to stay on at school until she was 11 years old, after which she worked full-time on the farm, growing mostly tomatoes that she'd sell in the local market.

Her sister got a licence for a stall in the main market in Ischia, where she remembers swapping a basket of grapes for apples, 'and that was the first time I had ever tried them!' Biggina also weaves her own trays – they look like rimmed tennis racquets with short handles – and in her retirement continues to sell these, along with foraged herbs and capers. 'It's how I meet people! What am I going to do? Sit on my own up here?' She has the most stunning views of the coastline and sea, so it would be understandable if that is what she wanted.

Rabbit was her family's main source of meat, only eaten on special occasions. Centuries ago, the islanders developed a unique way of rearing them called *coniglio di fosso*. They dig a 3 metre-wide by 4-metre deep stone-lined hole, like a well, where the rabbits are then able to make their own burrows and socialise as they would in the wild. Biggina also reared rabbits like this and grew the grasses to feed them.

Rabbit is an excellent lean meat, but you may prefer to swap it for six skinless chicken thighs on the bone. On the island of Ischia, this dish is commonly served with bucatini, a popular dried pasta.

Recipe next page →

FOR THE PASTA

275 g (9¾ oz) egg or 5 eggs
20 g (¾ oz) olive oil
500 g (1 lb 2 oz/4¼ cups) 0 flour,
    plus extra for dusting

FOR THE RABBIT SAUCE

extra-virgin olive oil
1 rabbit, jointed, including offal
    and head
4 garlic cloves
3 tablespoons chopped
    flat-leaf parsley
2 teaspoons finely chopped
    rosemary
1 teaspoon dried oregano
1 red chilli, deseeded (optional
    and to taste)
375ml (13 fl oz/1¼ cups) dry
    white wine
750 g (1 lb 10 oz) fresh
    flavoursome cherry tomatoes,
    or a tin of good-quality tomatoes
salt

Recipe continued →

To make the rabbit sauce, pour plenty of olive oil into a large casserole or Dutch oven and warm it up over a medium-low heat. Season the rabbit joints generously with salt and fry them a few at a time if it is a crowd to add them all at once; you want to sauté not simmer the meat. Once all the pieces all golden, return them to the pan. Add the whole garlic cloves, the herbs and the chilli (if using) and fry for another minute. Pour in the wine and let the alcohol evaporate completely (you can tell because the steam stops smelling boozy), then add the tomatoes. Add enough water to barely cover the meat and simmer it, covered, for 2 hours. After the first hour, taste the sauce and a piece of meat and if necessary adjust the seasoning.

While the rabbit cooks, make the pasta. Beat the eggs in a small bowl with the olive oil, then continue as for the usual egg pasta dough method described on page 11. Note: the addition of olive oil makes this dough softer. Leave it to rest, covered, for 30–45 minutes.

When the rabbit sauce is ready, roll out the dough to a thickness of about 2 mm (¹⁄₁₆ in). You'll probably need extra flour to smooth over your board and pin. Once you have done this, let the sfoglia dry for 5–10 minutes on your board; you don't want it sticking when you roll it up, and you don't want to keep adding flour. So: take some photos for Instagram! When you are ready, roll up the pasta as you would a carpet, and slice across it with a straight-bladed knife. Fettuccine should be about 5 mm (¼ in) wide – though Biggina wasn't bothered by width – and can be as long as you like; remember that those from Campania can be a bit thick or chunky.

When you are ready to eat, heat a large serving plate and ladle some still-hot sauce on it.

Bring a large pan of salted water to the boil, drop in the fettuccine and give the water a good stir to stop the pasta from sticking. Once the water has returned to the boil, cook the pasta for about 2 minutes before you nibble a bit. How many minutes it needs to cook will depend on how thick the ribbons are. When the pasta is al dente, scoop it out with a spider and transfer it to the serving plate. Pour more sauce on top, toss well and serve. Reserve the meat for the main course.

CLAUDINA'S DOLLARI

❖❖❖

SPINACH AND BEEF PASTA ROLLS FROM LE MARCHE

PREP	3 hours
SERVINGS	4–6

FOR THE RAGÙ

about 6 tablespoons olive oil
1 pork rib
500 g (1 lb 2 oz) braising steak
    in one piece
1 large meaty sausage
1 onion, sliced
1 celery stick, diced
1 carrot, diced
1 glass (about 125 ml/4 fl oz/½ cup)
    dry white wine
500 g (1 lb 2 oz) tinned tomatoes
salt

FOR THE PASTA

200 g (7 oz/1⅔ cups) 00 flour
110 g (3¾ oz) egg or 2 eggs

FOR THE PASTA FILLING

1.5 kg (3 lb 5 oz) fresh
    spinach leaves
2 tablespoons butter
400 g (14 oz) minced
    (ground) beef steak
pinch of salt
100 g (3½ oz) Parmigiano
    Reggiano, grated, plus extra
    to serve
plenty of freshly grated nutmeg

Eighty-four-year-old Claudina helps her son Ercole Moroni and husband John with the floristry courses they run in Le Marche. Dollari pasta was invented by her older sister after the war. This recipe has lots of steps but it's not difficult and makes a nice change to classic lasagna.

Claudina says, 'this ragù is a classic Sunday lunch. It will be delicious after a couple of hours of cooking but will be even better once the ingredients have settled down and got to know one another'. Consider making it the day before.

Pour enough olive oil into a large casserole or Dutch oven to coat the bottom (about 6 tablespoons). Place over a medium heat and brown all the meat in stages, so the pieces of meat don't steam. Remove the last piece of meat (the sausage, say) and keep on once side while you fry the vegetables in the same casserole for about 7 minutes until soft. Add a little more oil if necessary. Return the meat to the casserole and deglaze with the white wine. Season with salt. Add the tomatoes and enough water to barely cover the meat. Bring to the boil then reduce the heat and simmer, covered, for at least 2 hours. The braising steak will take the longest to cook, so you can take out the other meats as they become fork tender. The steak can be thickly sliced after 1 hour's simmer so it cooks more evenly. It will take the longest to cook.

On the day you plan to serve the dollari, make the egg pasta dough as described on page 11. Leave it to rest, covered, for 30 minutes.

Blanch the spinach in boiling, salted water for 30 seconds. Tip it out into a sieve over a sink, then let the spinach cool before squeezing out the excess water. It doesn't have to be completely dry. Put the spinach on a board and chop it finely. You should have about 500 g (1 lb 2 oz) of spinach.

Melt the butter for the pasta filling in a large sauté pan over a medium-high heat. Add the minced (ground) beef steak and fry for about 10 minutes until it has turned brown. Keep stirring and smooshing it so it breaks up into smaller pieces. Add the salt, followed by the chopped spinach, and sauté everything for a couple of minutes. Take the pan off the heat and stir through the Parmigiano and plenty of freshly grated nutmeg. Mix well and leave it to cool.

Recipe continued next page →   **MEAT & SEAFOOD**

When all the other steps are cooked and ready, roll out the pasta sfoglia to a diameter of 60–65 cm (23½ –25½ in); it should be 'see-through' thin (0.5–1 mm thick).

Spread the spinach mixture evenly over the dough and carefully roll it up like a carpet.

Bring a large pot of salted water to a simmer. Take a tea towel that has not been laundered with perfumed detergent and lay it flat. Otherwise, use a double-folded piece of muslin (cheesecloth) the size of a tea towel. (You can use cling film but it's not very planet friendly; but if it's all you have, use a toothpick to poke a few holes in it so the pasta comes into contact with the water.) Gently place the pasta roll along the length of it.

Wrap it up and tie it like a cracker with string. Lower it into the simmering water (if it has to bend a little bit, it doesn't matter). Poach the roll for 30 minutes, making sure the water doesn't go to a full rolling boil.

Carefully fish out the pasta roll and unwrap it on a chopping board. Let it cool slightly, then cut the roll into 2 cm (¾ in)- thick discs and arrange them on a serving platter. Coat the slices with spoonfuls of meaty tomato sauce from the ragu as you go. Pour more sauce on top and finish with a handful of grated Parmigiano. Serve hot.

The meat can be served as a main course with a green salad.

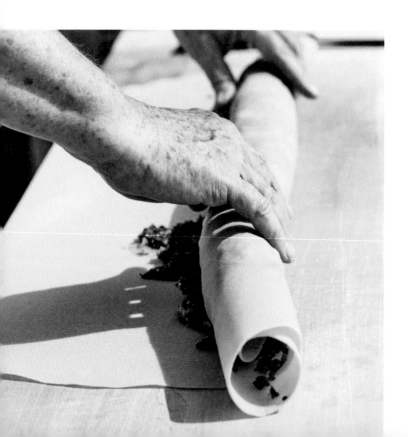

DELFINA'S FIENO DI CANEPINA

❖❖❖

ANGEL HAIR PASTA WITH RAGÙ FROM CANEPINA

PREP	2 hours, plus overnight resting time for the ragù
SERVINGS	about 8
DRIED PASTA ALTERNATIVE	Tagliolini

FOR THE RAGÙ

1 onion, roughly chopped
1 carrot, roughly chopped
1 celery stick, roughly chopped
50 ml (1¾ fl oz/3½ tablespoons) olive oil
200 ml (7 fl oz/scant 1 cup) dry white wine
150 g (5 oz) each of minced (ground) pork and beef steak
3 meaty sausages, casing removed and meat crumbled
1 teaspoon dried chilli flakes (optional)
1 teaspoon salt
2 pork ribs or shoulder, about 500 g (1 lb 2 oz)
200 g (7 oz) beef shin or stewing steak
2 x 400 g (14 oz) tins whole tomatoes
1 sprig of marjoram

FOR THE PASTA

300 g (10½ oz/2½ cups) 00 flour
165 g (5¾ oz) egg or 3 eggs

TO SERVE

100 g (3½ oz) mature pecorino, grated

Delfina has two passions: her *orto* (vegetable garden) and making fieno di Canepina. This little town in Lazio is surrounded by hazelnut groves (the nuts are all destined for a famous chocolate spread) but its yearly food festival, or sagra, at the end of October celebrates chestnuts; and the pasta served is fieno di Canepina. It's very fine tagliolini and Delfina – along with several other women – spends weeks beforehand making it. It's so fine it has to be dried first in a tangled nest shape, otherwise it would turn to mush when cooked. And so Delfina's spare bed is turned into storage space.

The ragù is typical of Lazio. In this region the philosophy is the more meats there are, the more flavoursome the sauce which dresses the fieno. The quantities below are for about 8 pasta servings because you need to make a decent amount for the best flavour. Serve the un-minced meats as a main course, and choose cuts which benefit from slow cooking.

Remember, you need to start this recipe the day before you want to eat it!

First make the ragù. Use a food processor to puree the onion, carrot, celery, olive oil and 50 ml (1¾ fl oz/3½ tablespoons) white wine. Place a large casserole or Dutch oven over a medium heat and add the mixture. Stir it around with a wooden spoon and once it has softened a little – after 7 or so minutes – and starts perfuming the kitchen, add the minced (ground) pork and steak, crumbled sausages and dried chilli flakes (if using). Stir well until the meat is no longer pink, then add the rest of the wine and season with the salt. Wait for the alcohol to evaporate, then add the other meats and stir well until the pieces are lightly coloured.

Crush the whole tomatoes; if there are any tough base-of-the-stalk bits, remove them, then tip the toms into the pot along with the marjoram. Add enough water to completely cover the meat and simmer very gently, with the lid on, for about 3 hours, until the pieces of meat are fork tender; then let the sauce rest overnight. Halfway through cooking, check the seasoning, adding more salt if necessary. Make sure there is always liquid covering the meat. Leave in a cool place overnight, or in the fridge if it's warm.

Make the egg pasta dough as described on page 11. Let the dough rest for at least 1 hour – this will make it easier to roll out. You want your dough to be transparent enough to read through, around 1 mm thickness. Let the sfoglia rest for 5 minutes, then gently roll it like a carpet into a loose, 3 or 4 finger-wide log; do not press down hard on it as you roll it, and try to leave some air between the layers.

Recipe continued next page →

Take a sharp, long-bladed knife and cut the dough into the thinnest tagliolini you can make. After you have cut a few strands, shake out and fluff them with the tips of your fingers to separate them. Keep the pasta well spread out on your board and let the strands dry a little.

If this seems a bit hard, roll your dough to the thinnest setting on your pasta machine and use the tagliolini attachment, though the result isn't quite as thin.

Use a sieve and scoop up the pasta strands to make a loose nest. Take a square of kitchen paper and turn out the pasta onto to it.

Let the pasta dry like this overnight at room temperature (on your dining room table or in the spare bedroom) before cooking. If you don't do this, the pasta won't be able to cope with the hearty sauce and it'll be a sorry muddle.

Be careful when you handle the pasta the next day: dried tagliolini are fragile until they hit the hot water and firm up.

Reheat the meat sauce. Use a large serving platter and sprinkle the base with a generous layer of grated pecorino.

Bring a large pan of salted water to the boil. Add the fieno a nest at a time. As the pasta is cut very thin it has a short cooking time – allow 60–90 seconds; more if you are using a small pan and the water temperature drops dramatically when you plunge all the pasta in it.

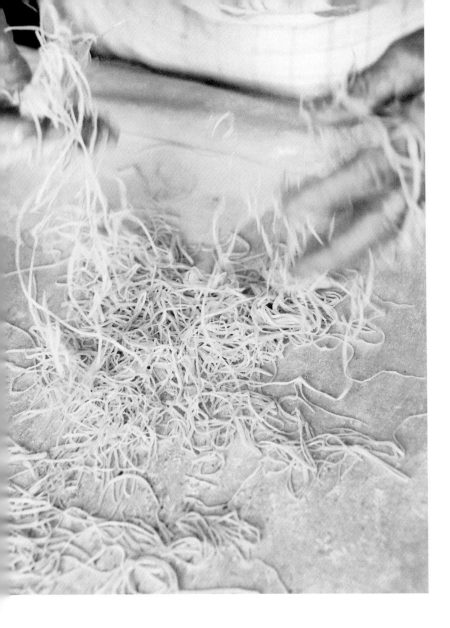

Drain the pasta well and place it onto the cheese-strewn platter, ladle a generous amount of sauce on top, add more cheese, then repeat with the other pasta nests. Toss the mixture well before serving.

If you are familiar with the video, you'll remember Delfina uses a towel to remove excess water from the pasta. If you do this, make sure that your cloth or towel doesn't have any perfume residue from the washing machine soap or softener.

ENRICHETTA'S RAVIOLI ALLA GENOVESE

♦♦♦

CHRISTMAS RAVIOLI FROM GENOVA

PREP	3–4 hours
SERVINGS	8–10 (makes 50 ravioli)

Sergio Rossi is a well-known expert and champion of Ligurian cooking and has his own TV show; he gets his love of food from his mother, 92-year-old Enrichetta. Her parents owned a trattoria which she helped with until she had Sergio and his sister. At that point, she took over a small pastry shop, which she gradually developed, at first serving savoury pastries and pies. Then, with her husband helping, they added fresh pasta and sauces. Sergio has fond memories of working there in the school holidays. Enrichetta was famous for her torta pasqualina and her shop, Trucco, was considered one of the best in Genova. She says, 'I don't eat out much, because I'm so critical. A dish has to be perfect'. And she's still cooking. These ravioli are labour intensive and only served at Christmas time, so she likes to make them ahead and freeze them. I suggest you do that too.

With regards to the offal in this recipe: it's a good example of 'nothing goes to waste'. If calves' brains and sweetbreads are hard to come by, you could use beef bone marrow instead, or ricotta. You will probably have to buy more brains than you need; in which case poach them all and your cat is in for a treat. Or mix it into your next meatloaf.

FOR THE MEAT STOCK

1 free-range chicken leg and thigh
200 g (7 oz) beef shoulder or any
   other stewing cut
2 celery stalks with leaves,
   roughly chopped
1 large carrot, roughly chopped
1 onion, chopped
1 bay leaf
½ teaspoon cracked peppercorns
1 tablespoon coarse sea salt
2 litres (68 fl oz/8½ cups) cold water

FOR THE SPICE MIX, BLEND THE FOLLOWING

1 teaspoon ground cinnamon
1 teaspoon ground coriander
½ teaspoon ground cloves
1 teaspoon ground nutmeg

To make the meat stock, put everything in a large pan with the cold water, bring to the boil then immediately reduce the temperature to a gentle simmer. Let everything cook for 2 hours, then leave it to cool before straining the stock of the meat and flavourings. At this point you can freeze it if you want. Otherwise, pour it into a clean pan and, when you are ready to cook the pasta, bring it to a steady simmer.

Mix the ground spices together; the quantities make more than you'll need, so save the rest for Christmas mulled wine.

Poach the brains and sweetbreads for the filling in barely simmering salted water (or a light meat stock) for about 30 minutes. When done they'll be a beige grey all the way through and firm to touch, let them cool and slice out any veiny bits. Set aside.

To make the rest of the filling, heat the olive oil in a frying pan over a medium-low heat, add the pork, garlic, bay leaf, rosemary and a small amount of marjoram and sauté very gently, adding some stock or water (enough to cover the bottom of the pan). Season with salt and simmer for 20 minutes or so until the meat is soft but cooked all the way through. Turn off the heat and let it sit in its juices until later use.

Cook the greens in salted boiling water for about 5 minutes until tender, then drain well, let them cool and squeeze out all the extra water.

FOR THE FILLING

50 g (1¾ oz) mix of calves' brains
  and sweetbreads
30 ml (1 fl oz) extra-virgin olive oil
200 g (7 oz) pork shoulder, cut
  into 2 cm (¾ in) cubes
2 garlic cloves
1 bay leaf
1 sprig of rosemary
1 tablespoon fresh marjoram leaves
400 g (14 oz) greens, such as
  borage, chard, chicory or spinach
75 g (2½ oz) day-old bread
150 ml (5 fl oz/⅔ cup) full-fat
  milk, for soaking the bread
15 g (½ oz) butter, melted
1 garlic clove
20 g (¾ oz) Parmigiano Reggiano,
  grated, plus extra to serve
½ teaspoon Spice Mix (page 156)
1 egg
salt

FOR THE PASTA

300 g (10½ oz/2½ cups) 00 flour
55 g (2 oz) egg or 1 egg
10 ml (⅓ fl oz) olive oil
95 ml (3¼ fl oz/scant ½ cup)
  warm water
a packet of candele pasta,
  or similar long-tubed pasta

Soak the bread in the milk for 3–5 minutes until soft and mushy, then squeeze out the milk and add it to a pan with the melted butter and garlic. Sauté over a moderate heat for a minute, then add the cooked greens and sauté for another couple of minutes. Blitz everything in a food processor to make thick green paste. Set aside.

Remove the rosemary and garlic from the pork and purée the pork pieces in the food processor along with the brains and sweetbreads until they form a smooth paste. Add the pork cooking juices if the mixture is too stiff and dry.

Combine both mixes together by hand and add the Parmigiano, finely minced marjoram, the spice mix, salt and egg. Taste and adjust seasoning as necessary.

Once properly cool, have another taste to make sure the seasoning is quite assertive – you don't want the final ravioli to be bland after all this effort. Put the mixture in piping (pastry) bag, if you have one, then stick it in the fridge until needed. Otherwise leave it in the bowl, cover, and chill.

Make the pasta dough as described on page 11.

Once the dough has rested, roll out the dough to a thickness of 2 mm (1/16 in). Enrichetta uses a pasta-rolling machine but you can make a sfoglia and cut it into 12 cm (4¾ in) strips if you wish.

Pipe shelled-walnut size dollops of filling onto the dough in a uniform row on the upper half of the strip (or use a teaspoon). Fold the bottom section of pasta over to cover the filling. Before sealing the edges, use your fingers to pat down around each raviolo to push out any air while also sealing in the filling. Use a knife or fluted pasta cutter to cut between each 'hump' to form a pillow –always leave at least 2–3 cm (¾–1¼ in) between each mound to be able to have space to cut between pieces later.

The finished ravioli can sit on the board for a maximum of 2 hours. They need to be turned over every 20 minutes until you cook them so that they won't stick. In fact, the best thing to do is put them on a baking sheet on parchment paper and freeze them in a single layer. Once frozen, you can decant them into a bag, seal the bag, and freeze them until you are ready to cook them from frozen.

Parboil 2 candele per person in a separate pan of salted boiling water (look at the cooking time on the packet and subtract 3 minutes). Cook the frozen ravioli directly in the broth, adding the cooked candele 2 minutes later after the ravioli have returned to a simmer. Continue to simmer for another 3 minutes. Distribute the candele, 2 per soup bowl, followed by however many ravioli folk want. Ladle over some broth so the pasta is just covered. Serve with grated Parmigiano to taste.

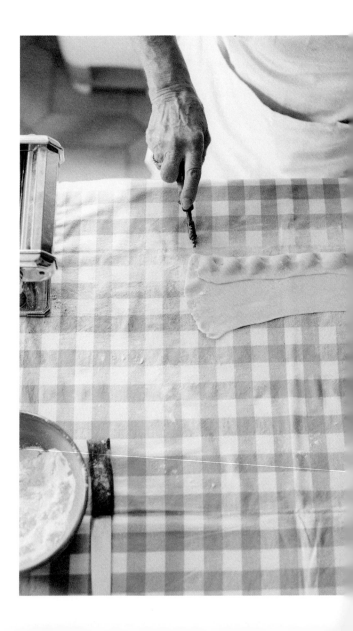

ERNESTINA'S CANNELLONI VERDI RIPIENI DI CARNE

◆◆◆

SPINACH CANNELLONI WITH MEAT FILLING FROM ROMAGNA

PREP	2½ hours
SERVINGS	6–8

DRIED PASTA ALTERNATIVE	Lasagna sheets

FOR THE PASTA

55 g (2 oz) frozen spinach
165 g (5¾ oz) eggs or 3 eggs
400 g (14 oz/3 ⅓ cups) 00 flour

FOR THE MEAT FILLING

175 g (6 oz) cow's milk mozzarella
4 tablespoons extra-virgin olive oil
150 g (5 oz) minced (ground)
   pork loin
150 g (5 oz) minced
   (ground) chicken
100 g (5 oz) grated Parmigiano
   Reggiano (preferably aged
   for 24 months)
150 g (5 oz) defrosted
   chopped spinach
nutmeg, to taste
salt

Ernestina is a bustling, smiling woman who seems to be permanently in an apron. She is used to working long hours. When her husband walked out, leaving her to bring up two small children, she had to take two jobs to make ends meet, one as a carer for the elderly. Now, at the age of 75, she continues to look after an elderly gentleman, who lives a couple of floors above her flat. Something she is proud to talk about is her third child from another relationship with a man she never married – and she doesn't care about the disapproval of some. 'It's my life; I adore my kids and I've worked really hard to support them. They are happy and settled, and that's all I care about.'

Ernestina makes cannelloni for friends and family and has a freezer full of them for emergencies. This recipe involves multiple steps but they are all straightforward.

Defrost the spinach, check the weight once drained of its water, and put it in a food processor with the eggs. Blitz until you have a uniform green liquid with no bits in it (bits will make your pasta sfoglia 'holey'). Double-check the weight of the liquid; it should be 220 g (7¾ oz) and if it isn't, top it up with water.

Make a well with your flour on your board and gradually pour in the liquid, mixing as you go, so you don't end up with rivers of green flowing off in all directions. Form a ball of dough – your board should be left quite clean as you incorporate all the floury bits – and knead it for 10 minutes. Cover and leave it to rest for a minimum of 30 minutes; it's fine to leave it for longer.

Dust a little flour over the board. Roll out the dough to form a 1 mm-thick sfoglia and cut it 15 x 11 cm (6 x 4½ in) rectangles to use for the cannelloni. This is a nice size, but if your baking dish (Ernestina uses a 30 x 20 cm/8 x 12 in dish) doesn't accommodate this length easily, calculate other rectangles to fit the width of your baking dish. Leave them on a tray, covered, while you make the other components.

Tear up the mozzarella and, if necessary, leave it to drain in a sieve for a few minutes. Heat the olive oil in a sauté pan over a medium heat, add the minced (ground) pork and chicken and sauté for about 10 minutes. Season the meat with a pinch of salt. Once the meats are cooked through, add the mozzarella, Parmigiano and spinach. Adjust the seasoning if necessary, and scrape some nutmeg into the mixture. Give everything a good stir and put to one side. The mixture should be nice and thick.

    Recipe continued next page →

FOR THE BÉCHAMEL

500 ml (17 fl oz/generous 2 cups)
  full-fat milk
50 g (1¾ oz) unsalted butter
30 g (1 oz) 0 flour
pinch of salt

FOR THE SUGO

150 g (5 oz) onion, diced
100 g (5 oz) carrot, diced
100 g (5 oz) celery, diced
2 tablespoons extra-virgin olive oil
300 g (10½ oz) minced
  (ground) pork loin
300 g (10½ oz) minced
  (ground) chicken
100 ml (3½ fl oz/scant ½ cup)
  dry white wine
600 g (1 lb 5 oz) passata
salt
30 g (1 oz) Parmigiano Reggiano,
  grated, for sprinkling

Now, make a sugo. Place the onion, carrot and celery in a food processor and pulse it until you have a rough puree. Cook this soffritto in a frying pan in the olive oil over a medium-high heat for about 7 minutes until the onions are translucent, then add the minced (ground) pork and chicken and a pinch of salt and stir until the meats are no longer pink. Deglaze with the white wine and wait for the alcohol to evaporate, then pour in the passata and enough water to cover the meat (about 100 ml/3½ fl oz/scant ½ cup). Simmer gently, covered, for 2 hours, stirring it occasionally.

Preheat the oven to 180°C (350°F/gas 4).

Spoon a layer of the sugo over the base of the baking dish.

Lay a pasta rectangle on your board and place a 2 cm (¾ in) cylinder of meat filling – which will look like an etiolated chipolata – about 2 cm (¾ in) from one long edge. Tuck this edge over the filling and roll it up.

Place the cannellone seam side down in the baking dish and repeat this process until the dish is full of snug-fitting cannelloni. You should have 16 cannelloni in 2 rows. Spoon a generous layer of béchamel sauce over the cannelloni, then a sprinkling of Parmigiano, followed by another generous layer of sugo. Lastly, cover the surface with more grated cheese.

Bake in the oven for about 25 minutes. If you like the top well browned, place the pan under a hot grill for 5 minutes.

Remove from the oven and let the cannelloni cool for 15 minutes before serving.

FRANCHINA'S FUSILLI CON GRASSATO DI CAPRA

◆◆◆

FUSILLI WITH GOAT RAGÙ FROM CILENTO

PREP	2–3 hours
SERVINGS	enough ragù for 8 people; pasta quantities are for 4 people
DRY PASTA ALTERNATIVE	Fusilli

Franchina lost her mother when she was nine years old; she died at the age of 43 from an embolism. As the eldest of five children, Franchina took on all the household duties, including cooking for her family. She had no idea how to make pasta and a kindly neighbour showed her how. 'You just have to get on with it, don't you. I had learn quickly.'

Franchina went to work on a building site; female manual labourers were common until the 1970s in Italy. Franchina's job was to be a human wheelbarrow and move cement. One day, the owner of the tobacco factory where she worked called her over. 'I thought, oh no! What have I done?' He asked her to step on the tobacco weighing scales; she was 48 kilos. The bag of cement was 50 kilos. 'We cannot have this,' said the owner and moved her to sorting tobacco leaves of which there were 5 grades. She was so nimble, she'd finish her pile and move on to help her fellow sorters. She finished her story with a smile and a shrug. 'I don't have much, so it makes me happy to help others.'

These days she is a widow who tends a collection of animals, a huge vegetable garden and 300 olive trees. She makes her own little goat's cheeses, which gently age on a hanging flat basket in her airy summer kitchen.

When we arrived for filming, Franchina had already prepared us a breakfast of potato and goat's cheese croquettes, deep-fried in oil over an open fire; she was totally unconcerned by the potential hazard, and they were delicious. The purpose of our visit, however, was to film her making fusilli with a goat ragú. Goat is a popular meat in the Cilento region where Franchina lives, 'but my kids don't like it. They don't like fusilli either, so I'm pleased to be making this for you'.

Traditionally, a castrated goat, reared for meat, would be slaughtered at home and one could not guarantee the blood had been drained from the animal properly. Thus, this two-step method of cooking the meat evolved to improve its flavour and tenderness. You can use mutton or lamb instead.

168 FOR THE BOILED GOAT RAGÙ

1 kg (2 lb 4 oz) goat meat,
 cut into 3 cm (1¼ in) chunks
1 onion, quartered
1 sprig of rosemary
3 sprigs of flat leaf parsley
3 teaspoons salt

FOR THE TOMATO SUGO

3 tablespoons olive oil
1 carrot, finely diced
2 celery sticks, finely diced,
 with leaves if possible
1 large onion, finely diced
1 teaspoon salt
100ml (3½ fl oz/scant ½ cup)
 dry white wine
400 g (14 oz) passata

PASTA

300 g (10½ oz/2½ cups)
 semolina flour
145 ml (5 fl oz/⅔ cup)
 warm water

TO SERVE

grated, aged goat's cheese or
 sheep's milk pecorino
diced fresh chilli

Place the meat, onion, herbs and salt in a large saucepan, casserole or Dutch oven, and cover everything with plenty of water. Bring to a simmer and regularly skim off the protein 'scum' which forms on the water's surface. Keep cooking the goat until no more foam forms and the meat is cooked; this will take about 45 minutes.

Meanwhile, make the tomato sauce. Heat the olive oil in a large sauté pan over a medium heat, add the vegetables and let them soften for about 10 minutes before adding the cooked goat. Season with salt, pour in the wine and let it evaporate before adding the passata. Leave this mixture to bubble gently for 40 minutes while you make the pasta.

Make the pasta dough as described on page 13. Roll out ropes about the thickness of a ballpoint pen. Snip cigarette-length pieces of dough. Place one under a ferro (square-sided iron rod) – or a bamboo skewer – and roll the dough around it with flat palms. Don't press down too hard, but be brisk as you move your hands back and forth. A tube will quickly form. Gently hold it in one hand and wiggle the ferro or skewer with the other to free it from the tube, then pull it out. Keep going until you have used all your dough and you have regimented rows of fusilli, drying.

Bring a large pan of salted water to a rolling boil then add your fusilli. Depending on the size of your pasta, it will need to cook for about 5 minutes. Taste one to judge its progress. Once cooked, drain the pasta thoroughly.

Remove the goat meat and serve it as the main course with a salad. Ladle the tomato sauce over the fusilli and toss them together. Serve with plenty of grated goat's cheese (or sheep's milk pecorino) and chilli to taste.

PAOLINA AND GIUSEPPE'S FRASCATOLE

♦♦♦

FRASCATOLE WITH LOBSTER FROM MARETTIMO

PREP	2 hours
SERVINGS	6
DRY PASTA ALTERNATIVE	Fregola

Set sail from the city of Trapani on the west coast of Sicily, and Marettimo is the last of the trio of Egadi islands before landfall in Tunisia. Here, Paolina and Giuseppe have run their restaurant for the last 42 years and they are just two of a seldom few who continue to make a pasta with very North African roots called frascatole.

Frascatole is a lumpy version of couscous; think granola. The traditional way of serving it in the winter months is with braised broccoli (boil the broccoli, then stew the veg in olive oil, with garlic and chilli). But, since the couple's home overlooks the sea and their son is a fisherman, they like to serve frascatole with lobster, which is plentiful in these waters. If lobster is too expensive or difficult to come by, then swap it for crayfish or prawns – even scallops would work – and adjust the cooking times accordingly.

It's important to allow time for the frascatole to dry properly, otherwise you'll end up with polenta.

FOR THE SHELLFISH STOCK

500 g (1 lb 2 oz) raw whole shrimp, crayfish or prawns
500 g (1 lb 2 oz) bony fish such as red mullet, scorpion fish, weever fish
4 tablespoons vegetable oil
2 litres (68 fl oz/8½ cups) water
salt

FOR THE PASTA

150 g (5 oz/1¼ cups) medium-milled semola flour
150 g (5 oz) cracked durum wheat grains for couscous (larger grains than semola)

FOR THE SOUP

20 ml (¾ fl oz) olive oil
1 onion, cut into 5 mm (¼ in) dice
2 celery sticks with leaves, sticks cut into 5 mm (¼ in) dice
4 garlic cloves, crushed
1 cinnamon stick
1 bay leaf
1.5 litres (50 fl oz/6¼ cups) Shellfish Stock (above)
1 tablespoon black pepper
2 teaspoons salt
500 g (1 lb 2 oz) passata
4 heaped tablespoons ground almonds
2 raw lobsters, halved lengthways

First, make the stock. Remove the heads from the shrimp, crayfish or prawns and peel off their shells. Keep the heads and shells for the stock and put the meat to one side for the main recipe.

Clean the fish, discarding the guts, tails and fins (it's easiest to ask your fishmonger to do this for you). Cut the fish into small pieces. Heat the oil in a large saucepan over a medium heat, add the shellfish heads and shells and cook, stirring constantly, for 3–5 minutes until the prawn debris wants to stick to the bottom of the pan. Add the rest of the fish and keep stirring for a few minutes, scraping the bottom of the pan to stop it from browning. Season with a teaspoon of salt, pour in the water, bring the mixture to a simmer and cook for 30 minutes (no longer, or the stock will have a bitter aftertaste). Strain it through a very fine-mesh sieve – a chinois – or through a coffee filter, to get a nice clear liquid. It's now ready to use.

To make the frascatole pasta you will need a medium to large, flat-bottomed earthenware bowl; a rounded one will make it harder to form the lumpy bits because the couscous mixture slips.

You need one hand to make the pasta and one to add the flours. So decide which hand does what in advance. Place about 200 ml (7 fl oz) room-temperature water in a small bowl and position it with the flour and couscous so you can reach them all easily.

Straighten your pasta-making fingers like you are gingerly holding a dog-chewed, wet tennis ball. Swirl with this hand, making sure all 5 fingertips touch the bottom of the bowl. While swirling, use the other hand to add small

MEAT & SEAFOOD

quantities of the flour and couscous, with splashes of water. If it doesn't come together, add a little more water. Don't worry that your frascatole balls are not the same size, but try and end up with something like looks like granola.

Spread the frascatole out on a baking tray and either dry it in the hot summer sun or put in an oven at 50°C/122°F until it's completely dry. This should take a day in Sicilian sun and an hour or so in the oven.

To make the soup, heat the olive oil in a casserole or Dutch oven over a medium heat, add the onion and celery and fry gently for 7–10 minutes until translucent but not brown. Add the garlic, cinnamon and bay leaf and cook for a few more minutes, then deglaze with the stock and add the rest of the ingredients, including the lobster, and let everything simmer for 10 minutes before cooking the pasta. You can tell if a lobster is cooked when the flesh is properly white not translucent. With raw shrimp, they turn pink, and this doesn't take long. Remove the crustacea while you cook the pasta in the soup. How long the pasta will take to cook depends on the size of your frascatole clumps, so keep testing it. Once it's cooked, return the crustacea to the casserole. Discard the cinnamon stick and the bay leaf before serving.

Ladle the mixture into warm bowls, preferably with a view of the sea.

MARIJA'S FUSI ISTRIANI CON SUGO DI GALLINA

◆◆◆

ISTRIAN CHICKEN AND PASTA

PREP	2 hours
SERVINGS	4
DRY PASTA ALTERNATIVE	Penne Rigate

FOR THE PASTA
300 g (10½ oz/2½ cups) 00 flour
165 g (5½ oz) egg or 3 eggs
3 g (¾ teaspoon) salt
5 g (1 teaspoon) extra-virgin
   olive oil

FOR THE CHICKEN STEW
6 tablespoons extra-virgin olive oil
2 legs and 2 thighs of
   free-range chicken
1 large onion, thinly sliced
leaves from 2 sprigs of thyme
leaves from 2 sprigs of rosemary
12 black olives, stones removed
3 garlic cloves
4 sun-dried tomatoes
75 ml (2½ fl oz/5 tablespoons)
   dry grappa (or brandy)
1 litre (34 fl oz/4¼ cups) water
   or chicken stock
salt (optional)

TO SERVE
handful of basil leaves (optional)

Eight-six-year-old Marija lives in Nova Vas, in the Istrian part of Slovenia, close to the Italian border, where folks continue to speak Italian alongside Slovene. And, where Italian is spoken, there's pasta – and here they make a pasta called fusi Istriani. Marija has been a garlic grower and picker since she was 10 years old. She is an expert braider of garlic ropes. 'I took these to the markets to sell them. Now I help my daughter in her restaurant and that's much harder work!'

For this recipe, Marija cooked a properly free ranging, three-year-old chicken; a supermarket economy bird will not give the same result, so try to find a good-quality one. 'We serve the chicken with the pasta because it saves washing up plates,' Marija says. I have adapted her recipe slightly, as she used a flavoured salt made by her daughter, and here I've added the olives, herbs and tomatoes, rather than ask you to make the salt first.

Make the pasta dough as described on page 11, adding the oil with the eggs. Leave it to rest, covered, for 30 minutes.

Roll out the dough to a thickness of 1–2 mm and cut rectangles about 3 x 6 cm (1¼ x 2½ in) with a straight-edge pastry cutter. Using a straight wooden spoon handle, take one corner of the pasta and wrap around the wood, slightly off-centre, but making sure the pasta edges overlap. It's a good idea to watch the video, as the action is much easier than it reads. You'll make shapes which look similar to garganelli or pointed penne. To seal each tube, grip and squeeze it gently with your hand and then, with the other hand, twist the spoon handle to release it from the pasta. Place them so they don't touch on a tray.

Heat the oil in a casserole or Dutch oven over a medium heat. When hot, brown the chicken one or two pieces at a time. Don't overcrowd the casserole or the meat will steam. Remove the chicken and set aside.

Add the onion to the casserole and sauté for a good 7 minutes until soft and translucent. Finely chop the thyme and rosemary leaves with the olives, garlic and sun-dried tomatoes, then add this mixture to the onion. Carefully deglaze with the grappa (it's more flammable than wine, so stand well back and if you use a gas hob, turn off the flame momentarily) and let the alcohol evaporate.

Return the chicken to the casserole and add half the water or stock. Cover with a lid and simmer for about 1 hour until the chicken is cooked. Check the seasoning halfway through; you may not need to add salt as both the olives and sun-dried tomatoes are salty. Add more liquid as needed, if the sauce is reducing too much.

Recipe continued next page →

Remove the cooked chicken and, when cool enough to handle, pull the meat off the bones in chunks. Put to one side, covered with kitchen foil to keep warm. Check the seasoning of the sauce.

Bring a pan of salted water to the boil and cook the pasta for about 2 minutes until almost al dente, then use a spider to scoop the fusi into the chicken sauce. Add the pieces of chicken and simmer everything for another minute or so, until the pasta is properly cooked.

Tear up some basil leaves and scatter over the dish. Serve with some Istrian wine.

GIGGINA'S GNOCCHI CON POLPETTINE E INVOLTINI DI MANZO

◆◆◆

GNOCCHI WITH MEATBALLS AND BEEF OLIVES FROM ISCHIA

PREP	4 hours
SERVINGS	5–6
DRY PASTA ALTERNATIVE	Cavatelli

FOR THE BEEF OLIVES (INVOLTINI)

3 slices of rump steak, about 70g (2½ oz) each
½ garlic clove, crushed
1 tablespoon finely chopped flat-leaf parsley
30g (1 oz) pecorino shavings
20 g (¾ oz) raisins
10 g (⅓ oz) Italian pine nuts
40 ml (1¼ fl oz/2½ tablespoons) extra-virgin olive oil
salt

FOR THE TOMATO SAUCE

1 small onion
½ garlic clove
50 ml (1¾ fl oz/3½ tablespoons) dry white wine
700 g (1 lb 9 oz) passata
3 large basil leaves
½ teaspoon salt
pinch of sugar (optional)

Giggina lives on the beautiful island of Ischia near Naples and she likes to serve this dish for Sunday lunch during the winter months. These gnocchi have a different potato/flour ratio to more northern variations of gnocchi (where it's a rule of thumb of 1 kg/2 lb 4 oz of potato and 300 g/10½ oz soft wheat flour); in fact, the use of semolina flour makes these more like cavatelli pasta than gnocchi – so remember to roll the dough into deep curls so it's not too thick. They are dressed with the meaty tomato sauce, and then the meatballs and beef olives are served as *secondo* with a salad.

Start by making the *involtini* (beef olives). Flatten the steaks with a meat mallet and season them with salt. Mix the garlic, parsley, cheese shavings, raisins and pine nuts together. Sprinkle a third of this mixture over one steak and roll it up like a carpet. Secure it with a toothpick or two. Repeat for the other two steaks.

Heat the olive oil in a frying pan over a medium-high heat. Once the oil is hot, sear the steaks one at a time on both sides until they are lightly browned. Remove them and put them to one side.

Now make the tomato sauce. Finely dice the onion and garlic together. Lower the heat under the frying pan to medium, add the onion mixture and sauté for about 7 minutes until it is soft and not browned, then deglaze it with the wine. Scrape the bottom of the pan well to gather as much flavour as possible, then add the passata, basil leaves and salt. Add a pinch of sugar, if necessary, and return the involtini to the sauce. Cover the pan and let everything simmer for at least 1 hour, possibly 2, depending on the meat you have chosen.

While the involtini cook, prepare the meatballs. In a large bowl, soak the bread in the white wine and mash it with a fork until everything is reduced to a pulp. Add the minced (ground) beef, grated Parmigiano, pine nuts, parsley, garlic, salt and egg and mix well with your hands until the mixture starts sticking together. Fry a small portion to test the seasoning and flavour. Adjust as necessary.

Recipe continued next page →   **MEAT & SEAFOOD**

FOR THE MEATBALLS

100 g (3½ oz) day-old bread
100 ml (3½ fl oz/scant ½ cup)
   dry white wine
300 g (10½ oz) minced
   (ground) beef steak
30 g (1 oz) Parmigiano Reggiano,
   grated
10 g (⅓ oz) pine nuts, finely
   chopped
1 tablespoon finely chopped
   flat-leaf parsley
1 garlic clove, crushed in a little salt
½ teaspoon salt
1 egg
vegetable oil and plain
   (all-purpose) flour, for cooking

FOR THE GNOCCHI

400 g (14 oz) floury potatoes,
   peeled and halved
250 g (9 oz/scant 1⅔ cups)
   semolina flour
plain (all-purpose) flour,
   for dusting
30 g (1 oz) pecorino, grated
   or ricotta salata, to serve

Recipe continued →

Prepare walnut (in-a-shell)-size meatballs by rolling the mixture between two flat hands. It's a good idea to keep your hands wet to help stop the meatballs from becoming sticky. Dredge the meatballs in flour while you preheat a small deep-sided saucepan filled 3 cm (1¼ in) deep with vegetable oil.

Fry the meatballs in small batches for about 3 minutes (per batch) until golden brown. Transfer them to kitchen paper to absorb any oil. If you prefer not to fry them, you can bake them in a hot 220°C (425°F/gas 7) oven for 15 minutes until browned.

Once the involtini are fork tender, add the meatballs to the sauce and cook everything for another 15 minutes.

Cook the halved potatoes in a pan of salted boiling water until properly cooked and there is no resistance when you jab them with a sharp knife. Drain them thoroughly, then rice or mash them, making sure there are no lumps. Dump the mash in a bowl, add the flour and work it into the mash. Mix and knead it gently only for as long as it takes for the flour to disappear and for the mixture to hold together without being sticky. If it sticks to your hands, add flour sparingly to not change the proportions too much. Cover the bowl and leave the dough for up to 10 minutes to let the flour fully absorb the moisture from the mash.

Cut off a small amount of gnocchi dough and gently roll it into a 2–3 cm (1¾–2¼ in)-width rope.

Cut squares from this rope and toss them lightly in plain (all-purpose) flour. Roll them down a ridged gnocchi board, being sure to flatten each one as much as possible so that the curl is deep and the ridges distinct. If you don't have a gnocchi board, a fork also does the job well. Repeat with the rest of the gnocchi mixture.

Bring a saucepan of salted water to the boil and add the gnocchi all at once. Once the water has returned to the boil, cook them for 3–5 minutes. Drain them thoroughly, transfer them to a warmed serving bowl and ladle over the tomato sauce. If one or two meatballs find their way in, so much the better. Use a spoon to coat the gnocchi in the sauce. Scatter over the grated cheese.

Keep the meatballs and beef olives warm while everyone demolishes the gnocchi.

IGINIA'S PRINCISGRAS

◆◆◆

PORCINI AND PROSCIUTTO LASAGNA FROM MACERATA

PREP	2 hours
SERVINGS	6–8

One can never have too many lasagna recipes! Princisgras is the 'town' alternative to vincisgrassi, a lasagna from Le Marche, specifically the province of Macerata. The latter is an end-of-harvest meal for farm workers and involves simmering chicken offal – including a stuffed chicken's neck – in tomato sauce, which is then used in the lasagna. I didn't think many of you would want to do this, so here is an easier, more elegant version.

As Macerata chef Iginia explained to me, 'Princisgras is an older recipe than vincisgrassi. It was invented by a chef called Antonio Nebbia for his wealthy clients and it is mentioned in his book, *Il Cuoco Maceratese* (The Cook from Macerata), published in 1774. I love it because he encourages women into the professional kitchen. The name is from *princis grasso* (fat prince).'

We've had to adapt this slightly; the recipe should include generous quantities of black winter truffles. The forested Sibillini mountains of Le Marche are a good source of them, so if you can find them, great; shave them as you layer the lasagna, over the béchamel sauce. This makes an excellent Sunday lunch.

FOR THE SAUCE

50 g (1¾ oz) dried porcini
4 tablespoons olive oil
200 g (7 oz) thick slices of
   prosciutto, cut into small dice
100 ml (3½ fl oz/scant ½ cup)
   dry white wine
black pepper

FOR THE BÉCHAMEL

60 g (2 oz) butter
60 g (2 oz/⅓ cup) plain
   (all-purpose) flour
freshly grated nutmeg, to taste
1.2 litres (40 fl oz/5 cups)
   full-fat milk
salt (optional)

Rinse the porcini in cold water to remove surface dirt. Place them in a heatproof bowl and just cover them with 350 ml (12 fl oz/1½ cups) almost-boiling water. Leave them to soak and rehydrate for 10 minutes, then take the mushrooms out of the water and chop them up into small pieces. Reserve the porcini soaking water.

Heat the olive oil in a sauté pan over a medium heat, add the prosciutto and fry gently until the meat just changes colour (over-frying the prosciutto will dry it out and make it salty). Deglaze with the white wine and, once the alcohol has evaporated, add the chopped porcini. Stir for a couple of minutes then carefully pour the porcini water into the pan through a fine-mesh sieve (to catch any dirt). Cook over a low heat for 10–15 minutes until the mushrooms are soft and the liquid has reduced. Adjust the seasoning with black pepper. Remove from the heat.

Melt the butter in a non-stick pan over a medium heat, add the flour and a few scrapes of nutmeg, and whisk until a homogeneous paste forms. Gradually add the milk while whisking and slowly bring to the boil. Keep whisking for 3–4 minutes until the milk has thickened and the béchamel doesn't taste like raw flour. Remove from the heat and adjust the seasoning with salt if necessary (the prosciutto is already salty) and more nutmeg. Your end result should have the consistency of pourable thick custard.

Recipe continued next page → **MEAT & SEAFOOD**

FOR THE PASTA

200 g (7 oz/1 ¼ cups) 00
  or plain (all-purpose) flour
100 g (3½ oz/⅔ cup)
  semolina flour
20 g (¾ oz) butter,
  melted and cooled
20 g (¾ oz) Marsala
  or Vin Santo wine
generous pinch of fine salt
135 g (4¾ oz) egg

TO ASSEMBLE

100 g (3½ oz) grated
  Parmigiano Reggiano

Recipe continued →

Make the egg pasta dough as described on page 11, adding the melted butter, salt and marsala to the eggs, mixing them together and making the dough as normal. Let it rest, covered, for 30 minutes.

Preheat the oven to 180°C (350°F/gas 4) and place a rack in the middle.

Roll out the dough to a thickness of 1–2 mm, then use a deep-sided 23 cm (9 in) round cake tin to cut rounds to fit it. Incidentally, a springform tin is helpful but not essential. Of course if your pan is square, make squares! You should end up with 6 rounds.

Bring a saucepan of salted water to the boil and have to one side a large bowl of cold salted water – allow 8 g (¼ oz) salt per 1 litre (34 fl oz/4¼ cups) of water. Blanch the pasta sheets in the boiling water for 30 seconds then transfer them to the cold water to stop the cooking. Drain well before assembling the princisgras.

Ladle some béchamel at the bottom of the cake tin, then place the first layer of pasta. Scatter the cooked prosciutto and porcini on the pasta (dot it about; think of it as seasoning, not a layer) ladle over more béchamel and sprinkle some grated Parmigiano. Repeat the layering another 5 times and on the top use only the béchamel sauce and cheese.

Bake the princisgras in the oven for 50–60 minutes, until the top is brown and crunchy. Remove from the oven and let it cool for 15 minutes before serving.

VARIATION You can play with this recipe; for example, fry 600 g (1 lb 5 oz) fresh diced mushrooms in butter and garlic, making sure all the liquid has boiled off, then add a scattering to each of the layers.

LUCIA AND FRIENDS' STROZZAPRETI CON FRUTTI DI MARE

♦♦♦

TWISTED SHORT TAGLIATELLE WITH SEAFOOD FROM SAVIO

PREP	1–1½ hours
SERVINGS	4

The seaside village of Savio has a yearly food festival, or *sagra*, to celebrate strozzapreti or 'priest stranglers'. This name is given to several different styles of pasta; here, they are twisted short ribbons.

The ladies in charge of making them for several weeks in preparation for the sagra are Anna Rita, Betta, Fenina and the matriarch, 94-year-old Lucia.

Lucia was born in the hills of Romagna. Her family were *contadini* (farmers), and she only moved to the coast when she got married. She brought some of her cooking traditions with her: she calls this shape lunghetti and she adds finely grated pecorino to the dough, not an egg. Eggs would have been sold and one only added them to pasta if they were surplus. Her friends smile and joke with her about her cheese preference, but for the sagra they prepare the following dough.

The seafood used for the dish depends on what the boats have caught, so make your own selection. On this stretch of the Adriatic coastline, mantis shrimp are highly regarded, for example. Prawns, clams, calamari and white fish are all good too. Don't choose fish like salmon or cod, which are not from the region.

FOR THE PASTA

400 g (14 oz/3⅓ cups) 00 flour
55 g (2 oz) egg or 1 egg
pinch of salt
150 ml (5 fl oz/⅔ cup) warm water

FOR THE SEAFOOD SAUCE

4 tablespoons extra-virgin
   olive oil
1 small onion, finely diced
pinch of ground cayenne pepper
1 garlic clove, finely chopped
500 g (1 lb 2 oz) fresh seafood mix
100 ml (3½ fl oz/scant ½ cup)
   dry white wine
300 g (10½ oz) fresh cherry
   tomatoes, halved
1 tablespoon chopped
   flat-leaf parsley
salt

Make the pasta dough as described on page 11 then leave it to rest, covered, for a good 30 minutes.

Roll out the dough to a thickness of 2 mm, then use a knife or pastry cutter to slice it into 1 cm (½ in)-wide ribbons. Pick up a ribbon and roll one end (a length of 10 cm/4 in) between your palms to twist it, then break off this section with your fingers and repeat the process until you come to the end of the pasta ribbon. Repeat with the remaining ribbons. Watch the video – it really helps! Place the strozzapreti on trays so they don't stick together.

To make the sauce, heat the olive oil in a large sauté pan over a medium heat, add the onion and cayenne pepper and fry for about 7 minutes until the onion is translucent. Towards the end, add the garlic; you don't want it to brown. From your selection of seafood, add the ones that need longer cooking time (e.g. cuttlefish). Add the wine and wait for the alcohol to evaporate, and if necessary a bit of water so that the bottom of the pan does not go dry. Add the tomatoes and a small pinch of salt and stir. Let this simmer a few minutes until you judge the squid or what you've added is nearly ready. At this point add everything that requires a short cooking time like shrimp and *vongole* (clams), and simmer everything for another 2 minutes. Remove from heat and stir in the parsley.

Recipe continued next page →   **MEAT & SEAFOOD**

Bring a large pan of salted water to the boil, add the strozzapreti and cook for about 4 minutes until they are almost done. Reserve a few ladlefuls of cooking water before draining the pasta well, then slither it all into the sauté pan to join the seafood.

Turn up the heat and give everything a good toss. If it seems dry, add a bit of the reserved pasta water.

Serve immediately, making sure to distribute the seafood evenly among the bowls otherwise there'll be arguments.

MARIA'S LASAGNA VERDE CON MAIALE E SALVIA

◆◆◆

PORK AND SAGE LASAGNA FROM FAENZA

PREP	3 hours
SERVINGS	4–6

DRIED PASTA ALTERNATIVE	Lasagna sheets

FOR THE PASTA

400 g (14 oz/3⅓ cups) 00 flour
165 g (5¾ oz) egg or 3 eggs
45 g (1½ oz) fresh spinach leaves

FOR THE RAGÙ

300 g (10½ oz) unsmoked
 pancetta, diced
1.5 kg (3 lb 5 oz) minced (ground)
 pork (loin or shoulder)
1.5 litres (50 fl oz/6¼ cups) beef
 stock
2 generous tablespoons tomato
 concentrate
600 g (1 lb 5 oz) blitzed whole peeled
 tomatoes (from a tin is fine)
3 garlic cloves
4 sage leaves
salt

FOR THE BÉCHAMEL

30 g (1 oz) unsalted butter
30 g (1 oz/3 tablespoons) 0 flour
½ nutmeg, grated
500 ml (17 fl oz/generous 2 cups)
 full-fat milk

TO ASSEMBLE

50 g (1¾ oz) Parmigiano
 Reggiano, grated (or more,
 if you feel like it)

Maria's YouTube episode went viral a couple of years ago and remains the most watched on the Pasta Grannies channel. Very sadly, she died at the age of 92 on 12 December 2021, a couple of months after we photographed her. She refused to stop working and insisted on helping her daughter in their little shop 'La Bottega del Buongustaio' in Faenza, pretty much until a week before she passed away.

In Emilia Romagna, a mixture of beef and pork is usual for this dish, but Maria said she always made it like this and, anyway, her customers preferred just pork. Given beef is more expensive than pork, I suspect there are a lot of housewives who make it this way.

Make a nice large flour well on a board big enough to accommodate your egg and spinach pasta sheet. Blitz the egg and spinach together in a food processor until smooth, then add the mixture to the centre of your flour well. Using a fork or your fingers, mix in a little bit of the flour from the inside of the well at a time so as not to break the sides and let the liquid escape over the board. Only collapse the walls once you're confident the goo won't run everywhere.

When the mixture forms a dough, knead it for 10 minutes until smooth and bouncy. Leave it to rest, covered, for 45 minutes.

Flour the pasta board and roll out the dough to a thickness of about 1 mm, then cut pieces to match the size and form of a 20 x 30 cm (8 x 12 in) baking dish. There is no need to cut rectangles only – you can cut to measure. You should obtain at least 5 pieces for this dish. Lay them out on a board and cover them with damp (unperfumed) tea towels so they don't dry out too much.

Now make the ragù. In a saucepan with no oil or butter, start by gently frying the pancetta cubes in their own fat. Once a good amount of fat has been released, add the minced (ground) pork, season it with salt and stir for several minutes until the meat is no longer pink. Deglaze with all the stock, then add the tomato concentrate and passata. At this point Maria would wrap the garlic cloves with the sage leaves in a small muslin square for later removal and add them to the sauce. As a cook, I usually think 'life is too short' when I read something like this, but do consider it, especially with the sage.

Recipe continued next page →

Recipe continued →

It is a bossy herb that should not be allowed to loiter too long in a sauce. Add the sage and garlic, wrapped or not, and let the ragù simmer over a low heat, covered, for about 1 hour, or until the liquid has reduced and the sauce is thick. Adjust the seasoning once more, and fish out the garlic and sage.

Melt the butter in a non-stick pan over a medium heat. Add the flour and nutmeg and swish with a balloon whisk until a homogeneous paste forms. Continue to whisk while gradually adding the milk and slowly bring it to a simmer. Keep whisking until the milk has thickened and the béchamel doesn't taste like raw flour. Remove from the heat and adjust the seasoning with salt and more nutmeg.

Preheat the oven to 200°C (400°F/gas 6).

Bring a large pot of salted water to a rolling boil. Have a large bowl of very cold salted water on standby. Blanch the pasta sheets in the boiling water for about 1 minute in batches, scooping them out with a wide strainer and plopping them into the cold water. This stops the pasta from cooking and makes the sheets easier to handle, quicker. After a few minutes, place them flat on more tea towels to drain.

Coat the bottom of the baking dish with a good amount of béchamel, as this will prevent the pasta from sticking. Form your first layer with a lasagna sheet, some ragù, Parmigiano and béchamel. Repeat until your last layer of pasta goes in, then finish with just a layer of béchamel and grated cheese. Maria liked to dot the surface with curls of butter, but this is up to you, it's not essential.

Bake in the oven for 45 minutes, reducing the temperature after 30 minutes if the top is already browned and crusty.

Remove from the oven and let the lasagna cool for 15 minutes before serving.

TERESA'S TAJEDDA SALENTINA

♦♦♦

MUSSEL BAKE FROM SALENTO

PREP	2 hours, plus 1 hour soaking time
SERVINGS	4–6

Teresa passed away on 4 March 2020, at the age of 92. Whenever one of our *signore* dies, it's like losing a favourite aunt, so even though she featured in Pasta Grannies' first book, I'm putting another recipe of hers in this one as way of saying '*addio*'.

We first met her as one of a group of lively women making tajedda for us. She stayed out of the hubbub and quietly got on with opening the mussels. And then it turned out she had a great sense of humour and was a whizz at making pasta, so of course we had to film her again.

Tajedda (pronounced 'tay-edda') is an all-in-one mussel bake which is popular in the summer months with families across the Salento region of Puglia. It has several spellings and multiple versions; this is the consensus recipe from Teresa, Lucia and Cecilia.

I have specified cherry tomatoes because they tend to have the best flavour when buying them in the shops, but if you have access to some luscious juicy 'country' toms, which have never been in plastic or a fridge, chop four up and use those. This is a *piatto unico* – a one-pot meal.

300 g (10½ oz) Roma or Arborio risotto rice
20 ripe cherry tomatoes
1.5 kg (3 lb 5 oz) live mussels in their shells
olive oil, for drizzling
1 onion, diced
500 g (1 lb 2 oz) waxy potatoes, peeled and cut into 5 mm (¼ in)-thick slices
2 courgettes (zucchini), cut into 1 cm (½ in) rounds (coins halved if using large courgettes)
dried chilli flakes, to taste
2 tablespoons finely chopped flat-leaf parsley
2 handfuls of coarse breadcrumbs
salt

Soak the rice in cold water for 1 hour. This step ensures the rice will be cooked completely after it's baked with the rest of the ingredients.

Cut the cherry tomatoes in quarters over a bowl to catch their juices, season the toms and juice with salt and put to one side. Rinse the mussels under cold running water and pull off their 'beards'. Discard any mussels which are gaping open. Take a short-bladed knife and prise open the closed mussels with a twisting movement of the blade between the two shells. Keep the half shell with the mussel upright.

Preheat the oven to 180°C (350°F/gas 4).

Take a deep roasting tray, about 30 x 22 cm (12 x 8½ in) and pour in enough oil to coat the base of it. Drain the tomatoes and keep the juices in a measuring jug, then arrange the ingredients in layers in the following order: onion, half of the sliced potatoes, courgette, tomatoes and rice. Lightly season each layer with salt, chilli flakes, parsley and a wee bit more olive oil. Finish with a layer of the remaining potato slices and arrange the mussels on top. Check how much tomato juice you have; if it's less than 200 ml (7 fl oz/scant 1 cup), top up with water then pour this over. Lastly, generously cover the mussels with breadcrumbs and drizzle with more oil.

Cover the tray with foil and bake in the oven for 30 minutes. Remove the foil and cook for another 30–45 minutes; how long will depend on the depth of your tajedda. Check for doneness by inserting the tip of a knife into the potatoes. The top should be golden brown.Remove from the oven and let it cool for 15 minutes before serving.

five

dairy

LUISA AND BERTA'S SCHUPFNUDELN

◆◆◆

SWEET OR SAVOURY POTATO GNOCCHI FROM SOUTH TYROL

PREP	1½ hours
SERVINGS	6

Luisa is a shy dairy farmer with five cows that she houses in an antique wooden barn through which chickens skitter, with cats patrolling the edges for mice. In spring, she moves them to Alpine meadows where the diet of flowers and herbs can be tasted clearly in the milk. From this, she makes 2 kilos (4 lb 8 oz) of raw butter a week, which she sells to Berta, the owner of nearby Hotel Saalerwirt, who is passionate about showcasing local produce to her guests. 'I like how you can taste the seasons in Luisa's butter,' she says.

The best way to appreciate butter like this is to spread it thickly on bread with nothing else, but dousing it, melted, over the local gnocchi called schupfnudeln makes them very special. If that sounds German to you, you are right; the women live just outside Brunek (or Brunico), close to the border with Austria. In this part of Italy, they speak a German dialect and Ladin, alongside Italian, and this is reflected in the cooking.

Traditionally, schupfnudeln was a sweet dish served with poppy seeds and sugar; the modern way is to serve them as a savoury dish with a shower of grated cheese – this recipe provides both options. Both need lashings of melted butter; try to source a cultured butter with plenty of flavour. And you can fry them too, so a nice brown crust forms, which is delicious. Incidentally, the Italian name for these gnocchi is *stringoli*, but neither Luisa or Berta called them that.

Schupfnudeln can be served on their own, and the savoury version as a side dish to game or vegetable stews.

FOR THE GNOCCHI
500 g (1 lb 2 oz) floury potatoes
2 eggs
2 g (½ teaspoon) salt
grated nutmeg, to taste
200 g (7 oz/1⅔ cups) plain
  (all-purpose) flour, plus extra
  for dusting

TO SERVE
100 g (3½ oz) unsalted butter
100 g (3½ oz) poppy seeds and
50 g (1¾ oz/¼ cup) caster
  (superfine) sugar, blitzed
  together or 3 tablespoons grated
  Parmigiano Reggiano

Preheat the oven to 180°C (350°F/gas 4).

Jab the potatoes a couple of times with a fork so they don't explode, then bake them in the oven until completely soft; this will take about 45 minutes – 1 hour depending on the size of your potatoes. Remove from the oven and, once cool enough to handle, cut them open and scoop out the fluffy potato: you'll end up with about 450 g (1 lb).

Pass the scooped-out potato through a ricer over a large bowl; this ricing gives the potato a lighter texture. If you don't have a ricer, you'll need to give them a quick mash, but don't go overboard; you don't want a smooth puree. Crack in the eggs and scramble them a bit, then add the salt and nutmeg, and mix them briefly into the mash. Taste for seasoning and don't be shy with it.

Add the flour to the mix and combine well, remembering you are not making pasta. Try to be light-fingered and speedy; if you overwork the dough, the gnocchi will be heavy. Stop as soon as you cannot see the flour anymore.

Recipe continued next page →

When the dough has formed a cohesive non-sticky ball, sprinkle it with a little extra flour and set it to one side while you scrape the board clean of any doughy bits – you won't want them in the schupfnudeln.

Cut the dough into 3 manageable chunks and roll each, one at a time, into a thick rope 2–3 cm (¾– 1¼ in) in diameter. Cut each rope into 2 cm (¾ in) lengths. Keeping everything well-floured, roll each piece between the palms of your hands, which should be perpendicular to each other, not in a 'praying' position. You are aiming for gnocchi with tapered ends so that they look like a torpedo. It will take a bit of practice but by the tenth one you should have the hang of it.

Bring a saucepan of salted water to the boil.

To prepare the finished dish, melt the butter in a small saucepan over a medium heat until lightly golden, but don't let it burn.

Add the gnocchi to the boiling water all at once, then immediately stir them gently so that they don't sink to the bottom of the pan and stay separate. After 2 minutes, remove one with a slotted spoon, let it cool a little then taste to see if it's fully cooked – it should not taste like raw flour.

Scoop the gnocchi out of the water and place them on a warmed platter. Pour over the melted butter and follow either with sugar and poppy seeds or the grated cheese. I have suggested Parmigiano, which isn't at all typical of South Tyrol. The cheese typical of Luisa and Berta's valley is Pustertaler, while the closest grana cheese is Grana Trentino; but unless you live in the area, you won't find them.

CARLA'S SFOGLIA LORDA

♦♦♦

MINI 'DIRTY PASTA' RAVIOLI FROM ROMAGNA

PREP	2 hours
SERVINGS	6

FOR THE BROTH

1 large onion, quartered
1 large carrot, cut in 3
2 celery stalks, quartered
300 g (10½ oz) passata
    or 4 ripe tomatoes
200 g (7 oz) flank steak
1 chicken leg
1 beef bone
salt

FOR THE PASTA

500 g (1 lb 2 oz/4¼ cups) 00 flour
275 g (9¾ oz) egg or 5 eggs

FOR THE FILLING

250 g (9 oz) cow's milk ricotta
200 g (7 oz) Parmigiano Reggiano
    (preferably aged for 24 months),
    grated, plus extra to serve
pinch of salt
1 egg, beaten
freshly ground white pepper,
    to taste
freshly grated nutmeg, to taste

'I HATE cooking!' Carla proclaimed to the ceiling. 'My kids will tell you my lasagna is really good. I don't mind making that. But honestly! Cooking is such a chore!' 'Perhaps you would like to share your lasagna recipe?' I asked. 'NO! Cooking it once a year is enough!' Carla grinned – her declarations were a bit of fun and I think she'll change her mind. She may be reluctant to admit it, but Carla is also famous in Faenza for her sfoglia lorda, postage stamp-size ravioli with hardly any filling.

Sfoglia lorda (or *spoja lorda* in the local dialect) originate from a little town just to the south of Faenza called Brisighella. The name means 'dirty pasta' in Italian, which gives you an idea of how generous you should be with the filling; it's just smeared thinly over the pasta. It was a way of using up excess cheese mixture for cappelletti – and when cooks had had enough of folding them up. The cheeses used vary slightly from cook to cook, but Carla's recipe uses easy-to-source ricotta and Parmigiano Reggiano.

This pasta is a whole lot easier to make if you can get hold of a ravioli cutter which simultaneously seals edges. It has a central metal cutting wheel with two outer serrated caps which are usually plastic. They are easy to find online and not expensive; just type in 'ravioli cutter and sealer'.

First, place all the ingredients for the broth in a large stock pot and cover them completely with cold water. Slowly bring to a simmer and cook for about 2 hours, skimming off any foam from the surface of the stock. Strain the broth and return it to the pot. Check the seasoning and bring it to a simmer.

While the stock simmers, make the pasta dough as described on page 11 and leave it to rest for 30–45 minutes.

Roll it out to a thickness of 1–2 mm (try to make it circular; trim it if you don't succeed and the edges meander, then it's easy to fold). Fold the dough in half and pat it gently, then unfold it – this will give it a central crease.

To make the filling, place the ricotta in a sieve over a bowl and leave it for 10 minutes or so to drain off any whey. Discard this then mix the drained ricotta in a bowl with the grated Parmigiano, beaten egg, salt, white pepper and nutmeg. Do not feel you have work to do with this step, as beating ricotta for ages will make it go liquid again. Just mix it, taste for seasoning and put to one side.

Recipe continued next page →

Smear the filling as evenly as you can over one half of the pasta with a spatula. Carla prefers the top half; you may prefer to the half closest to you, it's a question of habit not technique. Leave a border all around the edge so that you have some space to seal the pasta 'sandwich'. Bring the empty half of the pasta over the cheese half, matching the edges together. Pat the pasta all over, pressing out any air. Take a fine-pointed knife or a fork and stab the pasta at regular intervals. This is to stop air pockets from forming.

Now for the fun part. Take your ravioli cutter and run it vertically down the pasta at 2 cm (¾ in) intervals, then repeat this horizontally to create pasta squares. You don't need to separate them.

Use a wide spatula or flipper to shovel the sfoglia lorda squares onto a tray, then slither them into the simmering broth. Once the broth has returned to a simmer, cook for a minute, then remove one of the sfoglia lorda and taste-test it to see if it's done. They should be cooked in a couple of minutes.

Ladle them into warmed soup bowls with enough broth to cover the pasta. Serve with extra grated Parmigiano if you wish.

You will probably have leftover broth; use it for another soup or risotto.

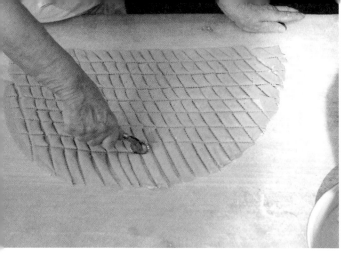

IRMA'S KROPFEN

◆◆◆

LEEK AND CABBAGE RAVIOLI FROM TRENTINO

PREP	1 hour 10 minutes
SERVINGS	6

FOR THE FILLING

⅓ head of savoy cabbage, tough stems removed

⅓ head of white cabbage, tough stems removed

1 leek, trimmed and washed

1 tablespoon butter or olive oil

200 g (7 oz) various mature cheeses such 24-month Parmigiano Reggiano, pecorino or mature Cheddar – anything with zing and bite

50 g (1¾ oz) fresh breadcrumbs

pinch of salt

FOR THE DOUGH

100 g (3½ oz/⅔ cup) rye flour (or wholemeal if rye is difficult to find)

300 g (10½ oz/2½ cups) plain (all-purpose) flour

a pinch of salt

about 200 ml (7 fl oz/scant 1 cup) warm water

TO SERVE

75 g (2½ oz) unsalted butter

6 sage leaves

DAIRY

Irma's family have an osteria, Albergo Rosa Alpina, in a hamlet called Palù del Fersina. It's 20 kilometres (12 miles) and a world away from the city of Trento. Pine-clad slopes give way to tumbled fields stippled with ancient apple trees. And dotted about are small farms, where dairy herds are husbanded and cheeses are made (of course) – the farmers don't bother to name their cheeses as their production is so small. Only sturdy vegetables grow here, such as potatoes, cabbages and leeks. So these ravioli are no surprise when you gaze down the valley over the village rooftops and survey this landscape. The surprise is that kropfen aren't better known because they are hearty, savoury and just the thing after a day's hiking.

Irma says only 10 people in the village make them. She is kropfen's champion and is determined this recipe should not be forgotten. When I visited her, Irma had collected the 13 different cheeses she says are necessary to make the filling – this probably has something to do with to the thirteen apostles, and using up all the bits and pieces of cheese which collect in the larder. Since Grana del Trentino, formaggio di Malga, Vezzeina and Montasio are pretty tricky to find outside the region, I suggest you gather your own collection of aged cheeses and make kropfen as soon as there's a frost outside.

First, make the filling. Chiffonade the cabbage leaves (i.e. slice them as thinly as possible) and cook the two batches of leaves in simmering salted water until just tender (how long this takes will depend on the cabbages you have bought, which in any case will have different rates of cooking, so it's better to cook them separately so you can judge 'doneness' better; it could take between 3 and 10 minutes). Drain through a sieve and continue to press the cabbage against the mesh to make sure as much moisture is removed as possible. You should end up with about 200 g (7 oz) each of green and white cabbage. Retain a cupful of the cooking water.

Chiffonade the leek, then soften it in a little butter or oil in a sauté pan. This will take a good 7–10 minutes over a low heat, adding a little cabbage cooking water if needed to stop it from colouring. You'll end up with about 100 g (3½ oz) of cooked leek. Leave it to cool while you grate your cheeses. Now mix them with the cabbage, leek and the breadcrumbs in a bowl. The cheese is salty, but the filling needs to be well seasoned: taste and season with a little salt.

Recipe continued next page →

Recipe continued →

Now, make the pasta dough. If you are using wholemeal flour, sift it first to remove any flakes of bran. Mix the two flours together with the salt in a bowl or your board, then gradually pour in the tepid water, mixing it in with a spoon or your fingers; you may not need all of it. You want a dough that is not sticky to the touch. Knead it for 10 minutes until smooth (it might take a bit longer if you're not used to this dough). Place it in a lidded bowl and leave it for 30 minutes.

Cut the dough in half so you don't work it all at once and dry it out. Roll out one half to a thickness of 3 mm (⅛ in) using a rolling pin. Cut it into strips 10 cm (4 in) wide, then 10 cm (4 in) intervals along the strip. Take one long side of the pasta and pull it over the filling to meet the other long side. Pat down between the bumps, trying to get out as much air as possible. Take a ravioli cutter and cut between the filling to create pillow-shaped ravioli. Repeat this process until you have used up all your pasta dough.

Bring a large saucepan of water to a gentle simmer and add a tablespoon of salt. Allow the water to return to a gentle bubble, then lower the kropfen into the water (you may need to do this in batches). Cook for about 7 minutes. Remove from the pan and place them on a platter, keeping them warm in the oven if necessary (if you're cooking them in batches).

While the kropfen simmer, melt the butter in a frying pan over a low heat and gently sauté the sage leaves for about 4 minutes until they are fragrant. Dress the kropfen with the sage butter and serve immediately.

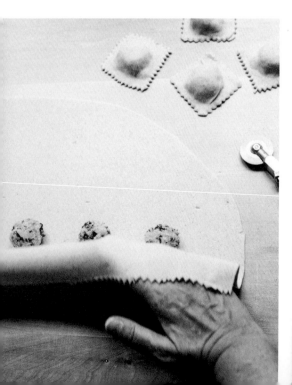

IRMA'S GNOCCHI DOLCI DI ALBICOCCHE

◆◆◆

APRICOT BUTTER-FRIED GNOCCHI FROM TRIESTE

Ninety-year-old Irma lives in Muggia across the bay from Trieste, right on the border with Slovenia. She worked for many years as a cook in a shipbuilder's yard, until it went out of business and she retrained as a massage therapist. She also found the time to be a scout pack leader. This is her take on susine plum-filled gnocchi which are popular in Trieste. Susine are violet skinned, yellow fleshed and a little bit tart; they have a short season and Irma liked the gnocchi enough to adapt the recipe. She makes her own apricot jam, high in fruit and pectin. When testing this recipe, we found that very un-Italian Seville orange marmalade also makes an excellent swap!

PREP	1½–2 hours
MAKES	36 pieces when each gnocco is 30 g (1 oz) each

FOR THE PASTA

560 g (1 lb 3 oz) floury potatoes
50 g (1¾ oz) egg or 1 small egg, beaten
a pinch of salt
150 g (5 oz/1¼ cups) 00 flour, plus an extra
40 g (1½ oz) for dusting

FOR THE FILLING

1 x 300g jar good-quality dense, firm apricot jam

TO FINISH

25 g (1 oz) butter
3 tablespoons dry breadcrumbs
ground cinnamon, to taste

A potato ricer is useful for this recipe. Place the whole unpeeled potatoes in a steamer and cook them for 25–30 minutes until tender. Place them in the ricer, and push through the mash onto a wooden board. Remove the peel that is left behind before ricing the next potato. You should end up with 500 g (1 lb 2 oz) of fluffy spuds.

Spread out the riced potatoes and leave them to cool for 30 minutes, then gather them together and form a well in the middle. Add the egg, salt and flour, then mix it all up to form a dough. Gently knead the mixture: all you are trying to do is incorporate the egg and flour, you are not trying to develop gluten, so once it's a uniform smooth texture, stop. Overworking the mixture will make the gnocchi dense. This should take 1–3 minutes, and you may need to use extra flour if the dough is sticky.

Dust the board with flour, cut off a section of gnocchi dough and gently roll it into a layer about 1 cm (½ in) thick.

Using a 6 cm (2½ in) pastry cutter or an upside-down glass or ravioli stamp, cut out rounds – with all the sections you will get 36 rounds in total, that each weigh about 30 g (1 oz); you may have to gather up and re-roll some dough to achieve this. Use a teaspoon to add a small grape-sized dollop of jam to the middle of the circle. Gently pull the dough over the jam to make a half-moon shape and pinch the edges closed, making sure they are sealed. Be warned, if you get jam in between the two layers, the dough won't seal properly, so avoid smears, runny jam juices, and adding too much in the first place.

Bring a saucepan of salted water to the boil, then turn it down to a low simmer and use a spider to lower the gnocchi into the water. Don't overcrowd the pan; you may have to cook them in batches. Gently swirl the water to keep them from

Recipe continued next page →

sticking to the bottom of the pan or each other. The cooking time will take 3 minutes when the water is gently bubbling.

While your gnocchi are cooking, melt the butter in a non-stick sauté pan over a medium heat. Stir in the breadcrumbs and fry them until they are golden.

Scoop the gnocchi from the water and place them into the butter in the pan. Fry them for a couple of minutes until they are golden on both sides. Finish them with a sprinkling of ground cinnamon.

This can be eaten as a treat at any time of day. You could also serve them with game such as venison.

MARA'S TIRAMISÙ ALLA TREVIGIANA

◆◆◆

TIRAMISÙ FROM TREVISO

PREP   30 minutes, plus overnight chilling

SERVINGS   6–8

Mara was taught how to make tiramisù by the chef of a restaurant called Le Beccherie in Treviso, which is where the dessert was invented according to one explanation (although in fact it was another restaurant in Friuli). As is often the case with these origin stories where a restaurant invents a dish, there are humbler, home-cooking habits and traditions which pre-date them. As Mara explained when she made this tiramisù. 'I remember as children, when we were over-tired and didn't want to eat anything good for us, our grandmother would make us a zabaione, but not the cooked version; it was just egg yolks and sugar beaten together. And it was a treat, a pick-me-up to give us energy.' In fact, when Mara's video was posted online, people wrote in from all over Italy to say their grandmothers did this too. It was a popular breakfast, some added milk, others coffee, and one or two nonne even put a drop of Marsala into the mix.

With this recipe, the eggs are not cooked, so please make sure they are free-range and from a reputable producer. Mara adds sambuca, an anise-flavoured liqueur, because she says it takes away the eggy smell. A more usual addition is Marsala, but you can experiment with any liqueur you have in your drinks cupboard. Or leave it out completely. Start making this the day before you want to eat it.

3 eggs
60 g (2 oz) caster (superfine) sugar
300 g (10½ oz) mascarpone
2 packets Savoiardi or lady fingers biscuits (exactly how many you need will depend on your dish)
2 tablespoons sambuca or other liqueur
500 ml (17 fl oz/generous 2 cups) freshly brewed strong coffee, cooled
25 g (1 oz) bitter unsweetened cocoa powder, for sprinkling

Separate the eggs into two large mixing bowls. Add the sugar to the egg yolks and beat with an electric hand-held whisk until light and creamy. Stir through the mascarpone until you have a cream. Beat the egg whites with a balloon whisk until they are stiff and when you lift the whisk from them, they hold their 'peaks'. Using a metal serving spoon, gently fold the whites into the cream.

Dollop a couple of tablespoons of the mixture into the bottom of a pie dish roughly 23 x 20 cm (9 x 8 in) and smear it evenly across the base.

Add your chosen liqueur to the cooled coffee.

Mara stipulates the biscuits should not be soggy with coffee, so arrange a layer of them, sugar side up, in the pie base, then use a teaspoon and carefully dribble coffee along each biscuit. Make sure you keep half for the next layer. Cover this layer of biscuits with half of the remaining mascarpone mix. Repeat with the biscuits and coffee, then add the rest of the mascarpone. Chill this overnight.

When you are ready to eat it, sprinkle the top with the cocoa powder. It should be nice and thick. Serve with some Prosecco.

RINA'S CAPRICCIO

◆◆◆

HAM AND CHEESE PASTA ROLLS FROM ROMAGNA

PREP	1½ hours
SERVINGS	4

FOR THE PASTA

200 g (7 oz/1⅔ cups) 00 flour
110 g (3¾ oz) egg or 2 eggs

FOR THE FILLING

450g (1 lb) fresh spinach leaves
300 g (10½ oz) sheep's milk
 ricotta
70 g (2½ oz) Parmigiano Reggiano
 (aged for 24 months), grated
1 egg, beaten
plenty of grated nutmeg
salt

FOR THE TOMATO SAUCE

400 g (14 oz) tin whole tomatoes
3 tablespoons extra-virgin olive oil
6 or 7 large basil leaves
pinch of salt
pinch of sugar (optional)

Eighty-seven-year-old Rina anxiously watches her best friend and neighbour, Cicci, pick some basil leaves for her. She is not sure she should have delegated the task because the plants, along with all the other flowering pots outside her back door, are her pride and joy. Cicci succeeds, and Rina relaxes. She has always had green fingers and a love of gardening. It comes from her childhood when she lived in Umbria. Her childhood tasks included taking the family laundry down to the river to wash, and bringing water back for household use, including for watering the plants. 'My mum had a lovely garden, with lots of flowers,' Rina smiled at the memory. The family moved to Faenza when Rina's grandparents' health started to fail and she was about 14 years old.

'We lived with them and my aunt. She was very proud of her Romagna heritage. She thought Romagnolo cooking was the best and we weren't allowed to make anything from Umbria. In fact, I didn't cook anything until I married Sergio when I was 20. We lived with my husband's parents and I used to practise making pasta after everyone had gone to bed so no-one would see if I made a mistake.'

These days, Rina has every confidence in her pasta-making abilities. She loves cooking for people and has a Sunday tradition of inviting her pals round for lunch. This pasta al forno called 'capriccio' is a favourite.

Make the egg pasta dough as described on page 11, then leave it to rest, covered, for a good 30 minutes.

Place the spinach leaves in a pan with a tiny splash of water, cover the pan and place it over a medium-high heat. Steam the spinach until the leaves have wilted, then tip them into a sieve over the sink. Leave to cool, then squeeze out all the water with your knuckles or the back of a spoon. You should end up with about 150 g (5 oz) of cooked spinach. Use a mezzaluna or a sharp, heavy knife to chop it all finely. Add this to a bowl along with the ricotta and Parmigiano and mix everything well. Season well with salt and several scrapes of nutmeg. Set aside.

To make the sauce, empty the tin of tomatoes into a bowl and use a vegetable knife (or any old knife) to chop up the tomatoes. Only the better-quality tomatoes go into a whole tomato tin, says Rina. Heat the olive oil in a saucepan over medium-low heat. Tear (don't chop) the basil leaves into the oil and leave them to wilt and infuse the oil for 5 or so minutes. Pour in the chopped tomatoes and let everything simmer for 10 minutes. Add a pinch of salt. You want a tart tomato sauce, so only add a pinch of sugar if you think it's too acidic. Set aside.

DAIRY

Recipe continued next page →

FOR THE BÉCHAMEL

30 g (1 oz) unsalted butter
30 g (1 oz/3 tablespoons) 0 or 00 flour
750 ml (25 fl oz/3 cups) full-fat milk
plenty of freshly grated nutmeg
salt

TO ASSEMBLE

200 g (7 oz) thinly sliced cooked
  ham (*prosciutto cotto*)
150 g (5 oz) fontina cheese, sliced
25 g (1 oz) Parmigiano Reggiano,
  grated

Recipe continued →

For the béchamel, Rina likes to make a paste with the flour and milk, adding the butter at the end, but the more usual way is to melt the butter in a non-stick saucepan and then stir in the flour. Beat the flour and butter a bit and let it fry a little for a minute or two to cook the flour, then gradually add the milk (which can be warmed in the microwave if you want). Season with plenty of nutmeg and a pinch of salt. The result should be like a thick custard in consistency. Set aside.

Roll out the pasta to a thickness of about 1 mm to make a 60 cm (24 in) circle. If you make a very thin pasta you can skip the blanching. If your pasta is a bit thicker, you will need to blanch it: bring a large pan of salted water to the boil and dump in the sfoglia, giving it a gentle stir to stop it sticking to itself. Leave it in the pan for a minute. Have a mixing bowl of cold water ready. Scoop the pasta out and dip it into the cold water to stop the cooking, then lay it out on a large tea towel or tablecloth and pat it dry.

Preheat the oven to 180°C (350°F/gas 4).

Smear the filling evenly all over the sheet of pasta. Arrange a layer of cooked ham slices on top of this, followed by a layer of fontina slices, then roll up the pasta into a log and cut it into 3 cm (1¼ in)-thick rounds.

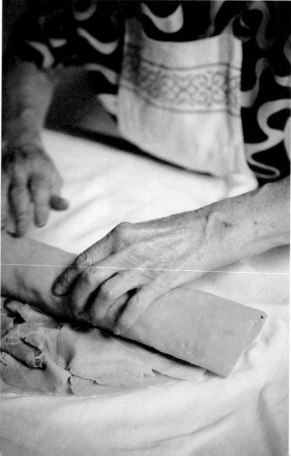

Prepare a 20 x 30 cm (8 x 12 in) baking tray by smoothing a thin layer of béchamel sauce in the base, then a sprinkling of grated Parmigiano. Use a spatula to arrange the rounds of pasta, cut side up, in one layer. Finish with another layer of béchamel, with some more Parmigiano sprinkled over everything. Lastly, add the tomato sauce in 'plops' on top.

Bake the pasta in the oven for 30 minutes if you blanched the pasta, or 40 minutes if you did not. Remove from the oven and leave it to cool for 20 minutes while you enjoy a glass of Spumante with your friends, then serve.

six

pizza, pastries & pies

ENRICA'S TORTA VERDE CON PRESCINSÊUA

◆◆◆

CHEESE AND CHARD PIE FROM GENOVA

PREP	2 hours, plus resting and cooling time
SERVINGS	12

FOR THE PASTA MATTA DOUGH

250 ml (8½ fl oz/1 cup) cold water
8 g (0.3 oz) salt
50 ml (1¾ fl oz/3½ tablespoons) extra-virgin olive oil, plus extra for greasing
500 g (1 lb 2 oz/4¼ cups) 00 flour or plain (all-purpose) flour

FOR THE FILLING

300 g (10½ oz) Prescinsêua (or 150 g/5 oz each whole-milk yoghurt and fresh curd cheese)
2 g (½ teaspoon) salt
40 g (1½ oz/¼ cup) 0 flour
750 g (1 lb 10 oz) Swiss chard with tough stalks removed (trimmed weight)
80 ml (2¾ fl oz/⅓ cup) extra-virgin olive oil
salt

Now retired, Enrica and her husband Gianni ran a small chain of takeaway shops offering traditional Ligurian street food like farinata, a chickpea-flour flatbread, and lots of different *torte salate* (savoury Ligurian pies). The most famous of these is torta pasqualina, an Easter pie with whole eggs added. This is the everyday version, with only 2 layers of pastry for the top, not the 33 layers representing the life of Jesus that have to be so fine they resemble Cirrostratus clouds of crunchiness. The dough used in this pie is called *pasta matta*, or crazy dough, because it's very soft and stretchy thanks to the oil and water.

Prescinsêua is soured milk (the cultures added are similar to yoghurt) which is then turned into a soft cheese by the addition of rennet. It's difficult to find outside the Genova area, even in Italy. You can make a good substitute by mixing equal quantities of fresh curd cheese with whole fat, plain yoghurt (preferably one with a bit of tang).

First, make the dough. Put the cold water in a large bowl, add the salt and stir to dissolve, then add the oil. Whisk well, then add the flour all at once and start mixing. Once the dough starts coming together, transfer it to a wooden board. Knead it by hand for 20 minutes. If it gets dry, dampen your hands with a little water, but do not add any extra flour.

Divide the dough into three equal pieces. Pat them into nice round balls, place them in snug-fitting covered bowls, then let them rest at room temperature for at least 30 minutes. The longer the better; in fact, beginners should let this dough rest for a couple of hours, as the extra time spent relaxing will make it easier to stretch it very thin, as required for this pie.

To make the filling, start by placing the cheese in a bowl and mixing in 20 g (¾ oz) of the olive oil along with the salt and 30 g (1 oz/3 tablespoons) of the flour. The latter helps to absorb any liquid released by the cheese and greens.

Chop the trimmed chard leaves and wash them in a colander. Spread them out on a tea towel and pat dry with another one. Damp chard results in a soggy pastry so be thorough about this. Scoop the greens into a bowl and season them with the rest of the olive oil, a pinch of salt and toss with the remaining flour.

Preheat the oven to 180°C (350°F/gas 4).

For this pie you will need a shallow 30 cm (12 in) pie tin. Pour oil into a small bowl, take a pastry brush, dunk it into the oil and thoroughly coat the inside of the tin, including the sides.

Recipe continued next page →

Start the bottom crust of the pie by rolling one of the three pieces of dough with a rolling pin, trying to keep it round. Once it's about 5 mm (¼ in) thick, watch Enrica's video. You are now going to emulate a pizzaiolo (a pizza maker), tossing and stretching the dough as you turn it. This is a great upper-arm workout.

Oil your hands up to the wrists and use the back of them to stretch the dough as thin as possible. If this is too tricky, keep the dough on the board, put both hands under it and use the tips of your fingers to pull and tease the dough larger and larger. Once it will comfortably cover the tin, lift it into place. Pat down any big air pockets. Spread the cheese mixture across the base to the edges, then pile the greens on top of it. Roll and stretch the second ball of dough, place it on top of the mixture, then brush heavily with olive oil. Repeat the process with the last dough ball. Take a pair of kitchen scissors and trim the 3 layers of dough, leaving about 4 cm (1½ in) of overhang. Twist and turn inwards both the top and bottom pastry layers to seal the pie. The shape is meant to resemble an ear, Enrica says. Brush the top pastry layer one last time with oil.

Bake the pie in the oven for 45 minutes. You should snip any air bubbles which form and baste the top with more olive oil halfway through to make sure it's very crunchy.

Remove the pie from the oven and let it cool completely before slicing it.

FENI'S PIZZA CON 'SCAROLA

◆◆◆

ESCAROLE PIE FROM PROCIDA

PREP	1.5 hours
SERVINGS	8

Ninety-seven-year-old Feni lives overlooking the marina on Procida, an island just off Naples. She is unconcerned by her lethally steep staircase, nimbly climbing up and down it without pausing for breath. And, rather than move, she now has a carer live with her, who painted her nails and did her hair for our visit. Feni wanted to look her best. 'I bought this dress for my trip to America three years ago to see my great nephew. I wanted everyone to be able to recognise me at the airport.'

Feni's version of *pizza di scarola*, or escarole pie, uses a non-yeasted pastry; the addition of lemon juice makes it crunchy which makes a good contrast with the soft filling. Escarole is a chicory which looks like lettuce and is only mildly bitter. Traditionally, Feni says, this pie would have been made with foraged greens, which are often bitter. If bitterness is not your thing, or you cannot track down escarole, then use Swiss chard.

FOR THE DOUGH

400 g (14 oz/3⅓ cups) 00 flour
 or plain (all-purpose) flour
200 ml (7 fl oz/scant 1 cup)
 tepid water
juice of 1 lemon (2 good tablespoons)
salt
1 tablespoon extra-virgin olive oil

FOR THE FILLING

700 g (1 lb 9 oz) trimmed escarole,
 chopped and rinsed
40 g (1½ oz) good-quality
 black olives
1 large garlic clove
4 anchovy fillets
3 tablespoons extra-virgin olive
 oil, plus extra for frying
½ teaspoon dried chilli flakes
 (optional)
15 g (½ oz) Italian pine nuts
40 g (1½ oz) raisins

First, make the dough. Have your flour ready in a large glass bowl. Whisk the water, lemon juice and salt together in a jug, so the latter dissolves, then add the extra-virgin olive oil and whisk everything again. Pour this into the bowl of flour and mix everything together with a plastic scraper to make a ball, before turning it out onto your work surface. Knead the dough for 5–7 minutes. Don't be tempted to use more flour in the kneading; it should be okay as it is. The result is a soft and elastic dough which should weigh 600–650 g (1 lb 5 oz –1 lb 7 oz). Divide the dough into two balls, one smaller than the other, say one weighing 250 g (9 oz) and the other 350–400 g (12–14 oz). The smaller of the two is for the top of the pie and the larger piece covers the base and sides of a frying pan. Shape them into tight round balls like you would for pizza and let them rest, covered, on your board for at least 20 minutes while you prepare the filling.

Recipe continued next page → **PIZZA, PASTRIES & PIES**

Recipe continued →

To make the filling, cook the escarole in a pan of salted boiling water for 2 minutes. Let it drain in a colander while you prepare the rest of the ingredients. Remove the stones from the olives – a cherry pipper is useful for this task. Finely chop the garlic clove with the anchovy fillets. Heat the extra-virgin olive oil in a large frying pan (keep the one you'll use for the pie) over a low heat, add the garlic and anchovies – with the chilli flakes if you are using them – and sauté for 2–3 minutes until garlic is fragrant but not browned, and the anchovies have dissolved. Add the well-drained escarole along with the pine nuts, olives and raisins. Sauté the mixture over a medium heat for about 5 minutes, until the greens are fully cooked and the filling is no longer watery.

Use a cast-iron frying pan roughly 28 cm (11 in) in diameter and 4 cm (1½ in) deep for the pie. Generously cover the base and sides of the pan with olive oil, so the pastry won't stick, making sure there is some in the bottom so the pastry base fries nicely. Roll out the large piece of dough to a thickness of about 3 mm, making sure that it will fit the bottom and sides of the frying pan. Spoon in the escarole mixture, patting it down evenly, then trim any excess dough hanging down over the sides. Roll out the smaller piece of dough to the same thickness and cover the filling like you would a normal pie. Fold over the sides of the lower pastry sheet to close the pie and use a fork to seal the edges.

Put the frying pan over a low heat and cook it for 10 minutes or so until golden. Then it's time to flip it. Handling a hot frying pan can be tricky, so slip the pie onto a plate, place another on top and flip it before returning it to the frying pan. Add a little more oil to the pan before you return the pie, and continue to gently fry it for another 10 minutes or so.

If flipping the pie seems a bit scary, bake the pie in the pan (cast-iron is ovenproof) in a preheated 180°C (350°F/gas 4) oven for 30 minutes. The pastry won't be as crunchy with this method, but it will still taste great.

FRANCESCA'S FOCACCIA GENOVESE

◆◆◆

THIN FOCACCIA WITH ONION TOPPING FROM GENOVA

PREP 30 minutes, plus proving and rising time

SERVINGS 6

98-year-old Francesca lives with several generations of her family. Like a lot of Italians, her reasonable-size house is divided into apartments that are home to her son and grandchildren. She still goes swimming in the sea (in a bikini) on a daily basis, though these days she doesn't like to go out of her depth as 10 years ago she suffered cramp while swimming and had to be rescued.

Francesca was a *contadina*, a market gardener, who had a stall in the local market. She still likes tending her vegetables and the onion for this recipe is one she grew. She says you should use the leaves as well, so as not to waste anything. If you cannot find fresh onions like Francesca's, use a red onion instead. Or serve the focaccia plain, which is the most common way in the Genova area.

Focaccia Genovese should be 2 cm (¾ in) thick, crunchy on the outside and soft in the middle. People eat it at all times of the day, even for breakfast dunked in coffee (not the onion version, of course!).

If you are swapping the 0 flour for plain (all-purpose) flour, make sure the protein content is 10–12% for this recipe.

FOR THE FOCACCIA

130 g (4½ oz) liquid sourdough starter, recently refreshed
30 g (1 oz) extra-virgin olive oil
200 ml (7 fl oz/scant 1 cup) tepid water
325 g (11½ oz/2¾ cups) 0 flour
10 g (0.3 oz) salt

FOR THE ONION TOPPING

1 large onion, including the leaves
generous pinch of salt
2 tablespoons olive oil

FOR SPRITZING THE FOCACCIA

1 teaspoon salt
3 tablespoons extra-virgin olive oil
3 tablespoons water

Two hours before you want to make the focaccia, refresh your liquid sourdough starter by stirring in equal quantities of water and flour. When you are ready, use electronic scales to weigh out 130 g (4½ oz) of the starter, zero it, then pour in the oil and 100 g (3½ oz) of the water. Add the flour and start mixing the ingredients while gradually adding the rest of the water. Lastly, sprinkle in the salt, then either knead the dough by hand for 15–20 minutes (or with a stand mixer fitted with a dough hook, for about 10 minutes) until it is smooth and stretchy. Should the dough be a bit too sticky and wet, stop kneading, cover the dough and wait 20 minutes before starting again (this will allow the flour to absorb the water better). Transfer the dough into an oiled container and let it prove at room temperature until doubled in bulk; this process can take hours and will depend on how hot it is in your kitchen and on the strength of your starter.

Roughly chop the onion and its leaves. Place in a bowl with the salt and olive oil. Scrunch it a bit and leave the onion to marinate.

Generously oil a 40 x 30 cm (16 x 12 in) baking tray.

Once proofed, transfer the dough gently into the oiled tray. Let the dough relax and, using oily hands, gently stretch the dough to fit the tray. If the dough deflates, don't panic, simply let it prove again.

Preheat the oven to 230°C (450°F/gas 8).

Recipe continued next page →   **PIZZA, PASTRIES & PIES**

Spritzing the focaccia helps to crisp it. Dissolve the salt in the water then whisk it with the olive oil as you would a salad dressing. Dip your fingers in this, then make dimples in your proofed focaccia. Sprinkle the onion evenly over the focaccia.

When the oven is hot enough, splash half of the water and oil spritz mix over the focaccia and bake it for 10 minutes. Take it out of the oven, sprinkle the rest of the water and oil spritz mix over everything and bake it for another 10 minutes. You may need to reduce the temperature if the focaccia starts browning too quickly. When it's done it should be crunchy on the bottom but still soft inside. Serve immediately.

NOTES ON SOURDOUGH   If you want
to make this recipe and would like to tackle
making a sourdough starter, begin the process
a minimum of 5 days before you plan to bake
your focaccia. There are lots of books, vlogs and
blogs dedicated to sourdough, which you should
read/watch if you are not already familiar
with the wonderful world of fermentation and
hydration. Essentially, you mix equal quantities
of a nutritious flour (wholemeal or rye) and
water to form a paste, and add the same every
day and until it starts bubbling. Keep the
starter covered with a muslin cloth at room
temperature while you do this. Or find a friend
with a starter, or order it online.

Francesca gave me some of her starter
(called *lievito madre* in Italian) much to my
alarm as I had never looked after one before
(I mostly eat bread as toast, where large holes
aren't helpful). I am happy to report it is still
going strong, despite being abandoned in the

fridge for several weeks at a time on a regular
basis. In other words, a sourdough starter is
a good-tempered yeasty beast, though of course
it prefers regular feeding.

Your liquid sourdough starter should be
nice and active for this recipe. This means when
you refresh it with equal amounts of flour and
water it should double in volume in less than
3 hours at room temperature.

If you are in any doubt about its vivacity,
give the dough a bit of a pick-me-up by adding
1 g of fresh yeast (or a heavy pinch of dried
yeast) to the 200 ml of water stipulated.

If you don't have a sourdough starter,
but want to make this focaccia, use 5 g (¼ oz)
of fresh yeast and use 390 g (14 oz) of flour
and 265 g (9½ oz) water.

If your flour is below 10–12% protein
(check on the side of the packet), then your
dough could be a little sticky, in which case
add a little bit more flour.

GIOCONDA AND BARTOLO'S PIZZA DA ISCHIA

◆◆◆

PAN PIZZA FROM ISCHIA

PREP	30 minutes, plus proving and resting time
SERVINGS	4–6 (makes a thin 40 x30cm/ 16 x 12 in pizza)

Gioconda and Bartolo live on the island of Ischia close to Naples. Their large vegetable garden and small vineyard can only be reached with a small car, a lot of determination, and cheerful acceptance of feral goats getting in the way of a first-gear zoom up the mountainside. The light is spangled, the blue is lapis, and it's no surprise their summer kitchen includes several bunk beds because no one ever wants to leave.

Gioconda has a passion for making brightly patterned aprons for her entire family, because everyone gets involved with pizza making, whether it's picking tomatoes or taking a turn with the pizza paddle. Theirs are not fancy Neapolitan-style pizzas but homey tray ones. Their oven, however, is a large wood-burning one, and the toppings come straight from the garden, so there is nothing ordinary about them. More important, though, are the good times had in creating the pizzas. This quantity can be doubled. Design your own toppings; their friend Luciana is allergic to tomato, so she does one with lots of herbs like rosemary and thyme, mixed with garlic, lemon zest and mozzarella.

FOR THE DOUGH

2 g (0.1 oz) fresh yeast
 (or 1 g active dried yeast)
150 ml (5 fl oz/⅔ cup) cold water
8 g (⅓ oz) extra-virgin olive oil
250 g (9 oz/scant 1⅔ cups)
 00 or plain (all-purpose) flour
 with 10–11% protein
5 g (0.2 oz) salt

FOR THE MARGHERITA TOPPING

200 g (7 oz) passata
2 garlic cloves, chopped
200 g (7 oz) fior di latte
 or cow's milk mozzarella
10 g (⅓ oz) basil leaves
30 g (1 oz) pecorino, grated
extra-virgin olive oil,
 plus extra for greasing

Dissolve the yeast in the cold water; if you are using dry yeast, let it sit for a couple of minutes until fully hydrated and the bits of yeast fall to the bottom of bowl. Add the olive oil and whisk it to turn it into a cloudy liquid. Pour this mixture into a large bowl, then add the flour to it. Mix the two together with a plastic scraper – this just helps avoid you getting very sticky hands. When the liquid is absorbed, sprinkle over the salt and continue to knead the dough until there is no dry flour left.

Turn the dough out onto a wood board and knead it for 5–10 minutes until it is elastic. Don't worry if it doesn't look smooth; it will be after resting time. If at any point it is too sticky, put it back in the bowl, cover it and wait 10–20 minutes. Use as little flour as possible, preferably no flour at all, during the kneading. After resting, the dough should be more elastic and smooth – if it isn't, knead for another 5 minutes. Shape the dough into a tight ball and let it prove, covered in a large bowl at room temperature, until almost doubled in bulk. Proving times depend on room temperature, but it will require at least 1–2½ hours.

Recipe continued page 242 →

After an initial rise, gently deflate the dough, patting it down, and use a rolling pin to roll it out to a rectangle smaller than a 40 x 30 cm (16 x 12 in) baking tray. Grease the tray generously with olive oil. Use the pin to help you transfer the dough into the tray and gently stretch it with your fingers to fit the entire tray. Place the tray in a warm spot and let the dough to rise until it has doubled in height. If you are using a round tray, simply keep your initial ball shape and roll it to a disc smaller than your tray.

Reheat the oven to 220–240°C (425–475°F/gas 7–9), ideally with a pizza stone in it; or use one of those tabletop pizza ovens that are popular these days.

Place the toppings of your choice on the pizza, trying not to crush and deflate the risen dough. I've given the ingredients for a Margherita; simply layer them in the order listed.

Areas that are not covered with ingredients should be brushed with a little oil to prevent the dough from burning or drying too much.

Bake the pan pizza in the oven for 12–15 minutes, checking the bottom crust for doneness. When ready, slide it onto a wire rack to keep the bottom crust from getting soggy.

Use scissors to cut it up and serve immediately.

ILDA'S CASINCÌ

◆◆◆

POPPY SEED FRITTERS FROM TRENTINO

Ilda's recipe involves several stages but it's well worth it! We visited her one snowy February afternoon. Her granddaughter and friends had come round to support Ilda (she's rather shy) and enjoy her casincì, which were gone in an instant.

PREP	1½–2 hours
MAKES	about 20 fritters

FOR THE YEAST STARTER

10 g (⅓ oz) fresh yeast
   (or 5 g/0.2 oz active dried yeast)
50 ml (1¾ fl oz/3½ tablespoons) milk
50 g (1¾ oz/⅓ cup) plain
   (all-purpose) flour (10–11%
   protein content)

FOR THE DOUGH

2 eggs (about 110 g/3¾ oz)
60 g (2 oz) ricotta
   (drained if watery)
1 tablespoon vanilla sugar or
   1 teaspoon vanilla extract
35 g (1¼ oz) caster
   (superfine) sugar
6 g (0.2 oz) salt
1 tablespoon dark rum
grated zest of 1 lemon
25 g (1 oz) butter, melted
250 g (9 oz/scant 1⅔ cups) plain
   (all-purpose) flour (10–11% protein
   content), plus extra for dusting

FOR THE FILLING

50 ml (1¾ fl oz/3½ tablespoons)
   tepid milk
6 g (0.2 oz) honey, e.g. millefiori
   or buckwheat
½ teaspoon vanilla extract
½ teaspoon rum
65 g (2⅓ oz) caster
   (superfine) sugar
65 g (2⅓ oz) poppy seeds
½ teaspoon ground cinnamon
50 g (1¾ oz) fine dry breadcrumbs
   (more or less)

First, make the yeast starter. If you are using dried yeast, sprinkle it over the milk. When it starts sinking, mix in the flour. For fresh yeast, dissolve it in the milk before mixing in the flour. Leave the mixture, covered, in a warm spot for 20 minutes to activate.

To make the dough, put the eggs, ricotta, vanilla extract or vanilla sugar, sugar, salt, rum, lemon zest and butter in a large bowl and whisk well to combine. Don't worry if you still see small lumps of ricotta.

Add the starter and the flour and mix everything vigorously with a sturdy spoon or your hands to obtain a soft ball of dough. Set aside in a warm place for 20 minutes to prove and double in size.

The dough is supposed to be sticky at this stage; don't be tempted to add extra flour.

Warm the milk in a pan and stir in the honey until it has dissolved. Add the vanilla extract and rum and give it a stir.

In a separate bowl mix the sugar, poppy seeds and cinnamon, then add your warmed milk and stir until a loose paste is formed. Gradually add the breadcrumbs. Set this aside for 5–10 minutes to let the breadcrumbs firm up the filling. Taste the mixture and add a pinch of salt if the saltiness of the breadcrumbs is not enough to properly season the filling.

Now make the casincì. Once the dough has doubled in size, turn it out onto a heavily floured work surface and roll it out to a thickness of 3–5 mm (¼ in). Make sure to dust the top of your dough with flour as well, to keep the pin from sticking.

Using an 8 cm (3 cm) pastry cutter or an upside-down glass of the same diameter, cut out about 20 discs. Place a teaspoon of your filling in the centre of each round and fold it over to make a half moon. Close and seal by pinching the sides together well so that they do not open while they cook.

TO FRY AND SERVE

sunflower oil, for deep-frying
icing (powdered) sugar

If they don't stick together, use a water-moistened finger to dampen one side of the circle before pinching. Make sure no filling spills out of the sides. This is a delicate process, so be sure you pinch the very outer border while being careful to not stretch the dough too thinly over the filling.

Leave your casincì to prove for another 15 minutes before frying.

While they prove, heat a deep pan of sunflower oil to 160–165°C (320-330°F).

Use a thermometer to test it has reached temperature, then drop in one or two casincì at a time and let them turn a deep golden or honey colour, then flip over once or twice to be sure they are evening cooked. This will take 2 minutes maximum – it's fast!

Turn out onto a tray lined with kitchen paper to absorb extra oil and serve warm with icing (powdered) sugar on top.

MARIA'S TORTELLI DOLCI DI CASTAGNE

❖❖❖

SWEET BAKED CHESTNUT TORTELLI FROM ROMAGNA

PREP	2 hours, plus optional overnight chilling
MAKES	30 tortelli

FOR THE CHESTNUT PUREE

150 g (5 oz) dried chestnuts
¼ orange, peel on
1 small slice of candied citron lemon
10 g (⅓ oz) caster (superfine) sugar

FOR THE ORANGE (CANDITO) SAUCE

the juice and peel (no white pith)
   of 1 orange (unwaxed)
50 g (1¾ oz) caster (superfine) sugar
1 tablespoon sapa, plus extra to serve
1 tablespoon dark rum

FOR THE FILLING

250 g (9 oz) boiled and puréed
   chestnuts (above)
Orange Sauce (above)
2 g very finely ground coffee,
   not instant powder
8 g (⅓ oz) unsweetened
   cocoa powder
50 g (1¾ oz) good-quality plum jam
50 g (1¾ oz) caster (superfine) sugar
grated zest of ½ lemon (unwaxed)

Brilliant pasta maker, Maria from Faenza in Emilia Romagna, is one of our 'star grannies' who is happy to be interviewed by TV crews from around the world. She has shared several recipes and this is her Christmas special: tortelli filled with chestnut puree, chocolate and jam, baked, then dunked in sapa. This is a sweet syrup made by reducing grape 'must' – freshly crushed grapes that still includes the skin, seeds and pulp. Sapa has several names, including vin cotto and mosto cotto and, while you won't find it in your local supermarket, it's available online and probably in your local Italian deli. Make the filling the day before you bake the tortelli if you can, as this improves its flavour.

First, make the chestnut puree. Place the dried chestnuts in a saucepan and just cover them with water. Add the orange and candied citron. If you don't have the latter, then add a tablespoon of marmalade instead of the orange and lemon. Bring to a simmer and cook for 1 hour or so, until the chestnuts are tender. You may need to top the pan up with water occasionally. Remove from the heat and let them cool completely, then drain them and pass them through a food mill with the fruit. This is the best gadget for the job because the resulting puree is fluffy; a food processor gives a denser texture.

To make the orange sauce, bring a small pan of water with a pinch of salt to the boil, then add the peel and blanch for 5 minutes. Discard this water and repeat the blanching step, but this time with unsalted water. Throw away the water and dice the skin as finely as possible. Return the skin to the small pan, add the orange juice, sugar, sapa and rum and cook over a low heat for about 5 minutes until thick and syrupy. Remove from the heat and leave to cool.

To make the filling, mix the cold pureed chestnuts and orange sauce together in a bowl with the other ingredients. You can now leave this overnight, covered, in the fridge. If time is not on your side, crack on.

To make the dough, mix together the flour, baking powder, sugar, zests and salt in a large bowl. Add the lard and butter (or just 60 g/2 oz butter) and rub the mix together with your fingertips to obtain a rough sandy consistency. Add the egg and knead the dough for 2 minutes until it holds together. If the dough has a hard time coming together, add a tablespoon of milk to help.

    Recipe continued next page →

Recipe continued →

250 g (9 oz/scant 1 ⅔ cups)
  00 flour
9 g (⅓ oz) baking powder
  (to make it self-raising)
100 g (3½ oz) caster sugar
grated zest of ½ lemon and
  ½ orange (unwaxed)
pinch of salt
25 g (1 oz) cold free-range lard
  (or butter)
35 g (1¼ oz) butter
1 egg, beaten
splash of milk, if needed

Cover the dough so it won't dry out in the fridge, and chill it until it is firm (1–2 hours). You can make this the day before, put in the fridge and remove it for 40 minutes or so before rolling out, to allow it to come to room temperature.

Preheat the oven to 180°C (350°F/gas 4) and line two baking trays with parchment paper.

Roll out the chilled dough to a thickness of 2 mm and stamp out 30 rounds with a 7–8 cm (2¾–3 in) diameter pastry cutter. Place a teaspoon of the filling in the middle of a disc and gently fold up the sides and hold it like a taco in one hand. Pleat a seam by alternately crimping one side over the other. Watch Maria's video to see how she does it! If this is too complicated, it will still taste the same if you make half-moon shapes with a simple pinched-closed edge. Repeat with the remaining discs and filling. Place each tortello on a lined baking tray, suitably spaced out.

Bake the tortelli in the oven for 20 minutes, until they are nice and golden.

Remove from the oven and when they have cooled a bit, pour some sapa into a small bowl and either dunk or brush them with syrup.

NICOLA'S SFINCIONE DI BAGHERIA

◆◆◆

THICK PIZZA FROM BAGHERIA, SICILY

Nicola's summer kitchen was a bakery. Now the wood-burning oven is used for sfincione family feasts. Sfincione are thick pizzas and there are two kinds: a tomato topping is typical of Palermo, whereas the 'white' no-tomato versions are typical of Bagheria, a seaside town just to the east of Palermo. Nicola says these were traditionally made over the Christmas holidays when fresh green scalogno onions are available. These are called spring onions in the UK and scallions in America. You could also use leeks, which is not typical but gives the sfincione a similar taste. Primo sale is a young cheese – the name translates as 'first salt' – which can be made from cow's or sheep's milk. It melts easily and is rich in fat. Most Italian delis should have it.

PREP	1 hour, plus proving and resting time
SERVINGS	2 x 20 cm (8 in) sfincione (8–12 slices)

FOR THE DOUGH

5 g (0.2 oz) fresh yeast
   (or 3 g/0.1 oz active dried yeast)
350 ml (12 fl oz/1½ cups)
   cold water
10 g (⅓ oz) sugar
12 g (0.4 oz) extra-virgin olive oil
500 g (1 lb 2 oz/4¼ cups) semolina
   flour (*semola rimacinata*)
12 g (0.4 oz) salt
0 or 00 flour, for dusting

FOR THE COOKED ONIONS

350 g (12 oz) trimmed large spring
   onions (scallions)
50 ml (1¾ fl oz/3½ tablespoons)
   olive oil
½ teaspoon salt
100 ml (3½ fl oz/scant ½ cup)
   water, plus extra if needed

FOR THE BREADCRUMB MIX

250 g (9 oz) fresh white bread
   (crusts removed)
75 g (2½ oz) grated caciocavallo
   or unsmoked scamorza cheese
1 teaspoon salt
3 teaspoons dried oregano
3 spring onions (scallions), sliced
75 ml (2½ fl oz/5 tablespoons)
   olive oil, plus extra if needed
   (depending on your breadcrumbs)

Dissolve the yeast in the cold water; if you are using dried yeast, let it sit a few minutes, then whisk. Add the sugar to the water and whisk again to dissolve. Add the oil to the water followed by all the flour and start combining it with your hands or a dough scraper. Once the water is absorbed, add the salt.

Start kneading the dough in the bowl for ease then, once it is no longer sticky and all flour is incorporated, turn it out on your work surface to knead it further. Don't be tempted to add more flour while kneading. If the dough is wet, place it back in your bowl and cover it with a lid for 10–20 minutes to allow the flour to absorb more of the water. It should be easier to work after that.

If you know how to use the 'slap and fold' method of bread-making, this will help the process and you'll find you'll need little to no extra flour. If kneading only by hand, be prepared to use the extra flour indicated above to dust your hands and surface to obtain a soft elastic dough. (If you'd rather use a stand mixer, use the dough hook on the slowest speed and it will take about 5 minutes.) Working with hard wheat requires patience because the water is absorbed slowly by its starch and protein. Overall, you will need a couple of pauses and a total active kneading time of 10–15 minutes.

Place the dough back in the bowl and let it prove (covered) until doubled in bulk. It will take about 2 hours if kept in a warm spot, and up to 4 hours if kept at normal room temperature (20–24°C/68–75°F).

At this point, divide the dough in half and, without completely deflating them, form two balls of dough. Place them onto a tray lined with parchment paper and let them prove, covered, until doubled in size. This time, the proving time should be shorter, between 1–2 hours.

Recipe continued next page →

FOR THE TOPPING

25 g (1 oz) salted anchovy fillets, rinsed and roughly chopped
125 g (4 oz) primo sale, cut into 2 mm (¹⁄₁₆ in)-thick slices

To prepare the spring onions (scallions), cut them in half lengthways. If they are small you can cut them in quarters, otherwise cut them finely crossways. Place them in a pan along with the oil, salt and water. Cook over a low heat for about 20 minutes until very soft, adding more water if necessary to prevent the onions from caramelising. Set aside and let cool – do not discard the cooking oil as it can be added to the breadcrumbs.

Now make the breadcrumb mixture in a bowl. Crumble the bread and rub it through a cheese grater's large holes. Add the grated cheese, season with the salt, oregano and onions. Drizzle the olive oil over it. Toss well to combine all the ingredients.

Preheat the oven to 250°C (490°F/gas 9), if you have a pizza stone, place it in the oven to mimic Nicola's hot wood-fired oven.

With your risen balls of dough still on their parchment paper, sprinkle them with flour and flatten them gently being careful to avoid crushing the edges of the dough – they should be about 5 mm (¼ in) thick. Now layer up your sfincione! Spread your roughly chopped or shredded anchovies over the top and arrange the primo sale so that it covers the sfincione leaving a 1 cm (½ in) edge. Add a very generous amount of cooked onions over the top of the cheese; the final layer is a heaping amount of the breadcrumb mix to cover the whole 'pizza'.

Transfer the sfincione still on parchment paper onto a baking sheet and then into the oven. Reduce the temperature to 200°C (400°F/gas 6) and cook for about 30 minutes. If the breadcrumbs are getting too dark too fast, reduce the temperature again to 180°C (350°F/gas 4).

If you have a pizza peel you can transfer the sfincione directly onto the pizza stone after the first 15 minutes of baking – this will result in a crunchier bottom crust.

Have assembled a ravenous crowd of people to eat them immediately.

PIZZICOTTI

◆◆◆

PIZZA DOUGH BALLS WITH CHILLI AND GARLIC

PREP	1½ hours
SERVINGS	6

FOR THE DOUGH

500 g (1 lb 2 oz/4¼ cups)
  plain (all-purpose) flour
  (10% protein), plus extra
  for dusting
10 g (⅓ oz) salt
2 g (0.1 oz) fresh yeast
  (or 1 g dried yeast)
300 ml (10 fl oz/1¼ cups)
  cold water
olive oil, for greasing the bowl

FOR THE CONDIMENT

2 plump garlic cloves
plenty of extra-virgin olive oil
1 teaspoon dried chilli flakes,
  or to taste

Quite a lot goes on behind the scenes before we meet the women we film, and they can decline at any time. Usually it's an instant 'no', and that's fine. On this occasion, we'd made it to the mountains of Abruzzo which border Lazio, trudged through frost-hardened snow to our signora's front door and set up the cameras in her kitchen, when she announced she didn't want her face on video. So there is no episode but this recipe is too simple and moreish not to share.

Pizzicotti, the story goes, are what Abruzzese farm workers used to have for breakfast. Raw bread dough, collected from the communal bakery, is turned into gnocchi-sized bits, boiled (because most houses didn't have an oven) and fried with plenty of olive oil, chopped garlic and chilli flakes. There. That's it. I suggest you save some of your dough from the other recipes in this chapter and try it. If you want to start from scratch, here is the recipe.

Mix the flour and salt together in a large bowl. Dissolve the yeast in the water then pour it into the flour and salt mix. Use a spatula or a spoon and mix the water into the flour until it all comes together as a shaggy muddle. Flour your working surface well and transfer the dough to it. Knead it for 10–15 minutes, until the dough is silky and elastic.

Place the dough in a well-oiled bowl, cover with a tea towel, and leave at room temperature until it has doubled in bulk. Depending on your kitchen temperature, this will take about 1 hour.

When you are ready to eat, finely chop the garlic cloves. Add enough olive oil to cover the base of a sauté pan and add the garlic and chilli flakes. Heat the pan up slowly and don't let the garlic brown. Turn off the heat and keep the chilli-garlic oil handy for the final step.

Bring a saucepan of salted water to the boil.

In the meantime, keeping everything well floured, take the dough and pull off a handful. Roll it into a chunky rope and, using a dough scraper, cut the rope into shelled-walnut-size pieces. Repeat with the rest of the dough.

Once the water has come to the boil, drop the dough bits into the pan. Don't overcrowd the pan and cook them in batches if necessary. Start tasting after about 1 minute to see how well the pizzicotti are cooked through. You should not have a raw centre or the taste of raw flour. Once the pizzicotti are done, turn the heat under the frying pan up to medium, use a sieve to scoop the pizzicotti out and toss them in the garlic and chilli mix.

Serve hot!

THANK YOU

Writing a book is always a group effort, and first and foremost I'd like to thank all the open-hearted and lovely women (and the occasional man) and their families who invite us into their homes to share their recipes. Please head on over to Pasta Grannies YouTube channel to meet them all; alas we only have space for a few of them in this book. Thanks to all the people who help me with the channel: Livia De Giovanna, Andrea Neri, Luis Carballo, Amanda Vila-Lobos, Heliana Trovato, Charlie Williams, Gerry Diebel. Thank you to everyone who has helped us along the way, including Sergio Rossi, Karima Moyer Nocchi, Letitia Clark, Nick Gibba and Michelle Lovric.

Thanks to Julia Griner and Pino Ficara for testing all the recipes, my agent, Ariella Feiner of United Agents, and to all the Hardie Grant team: Kajal Mistry, Emma Hopkin, Eve Marleau, Harriet Thornley, Valentina Coppo, Lizzie Mayson, Kitty Coles and Emma Lee.

Lastly thanks to my 90 year old mother Sue Bennison who is still cooking and playing tennis; and my husband Billy Macqueen whose presence makes all my adventures fun.

Published in 2022 by Hardie Grant Books,
an imprint of Hardie Grant Publishing

Hardie Grant Books (London)
5th & 6th Floors
52–54 Southwark Street
London SE1 1UN

Hardie Grant Books (Melbourne)
Building 1, 658 Church Street
Richmond, Victoria 3121

hardiegrantbooks.com

British Library Cataloguing-in-Publication Data.
A catalogue record for this book is available
from the British Library.

Pasta Grannies Comfort Cooking
ISBN: 978-1-78488-524-3

10 9 8 7 6 5 4 3 2 1

Publishing Director: Kajal Mistry
Acting Publishing Director: Emma Hopkin
Copy Editor: Laura Nickoll
Food and Prop Stylist: Kitty Coles
Art Direction & Design: Susan Le | Evi-O.Studio
Illustration & Design Assistant: Katherine Zhang |
Evi-O.Studio
Production Controller: Nikolaus Ginelli

Colour reproduction by F1.
Printed and bound in China
by Leo Paper Products Ltd.

MIX
Paper from
responsible sources
FSC™ C020056